UNCAUGHT

UNCAUGHT

A Practical Guide
to Escaping the TRAP of Offense

Rob Coburn

Total Fusion Press

UnCaught: A Practical Guide to Expecting Offense
Published by Total Fusion Press
Strasburg, Ohio

I would like to express my deep gratitude to Pastor Duane Sheriff and His team for granting us the ability to use phraseology and content from some of His teachings in the writing of this book.

ISBN (paperback): 978-1-943496-23-5
ISBN (ebook): 978-1-943496-24-2

Cover design: Josh Aul at NexLevel Design (
Editor: Kara Starcher at Mountain Creek Books (mountaincreekbooks.com)

Published in Association with Total Fusion Ministries, Strasburg, OH.
www.totalfusionministries.org

To my rock and sweetheart, Jen.
Your constant support has meant the world to me as I dove into the wild world of overcoming offense. Thanks for being my partner in this adventure.

To my awesome daughters, Caitlyn and Kylee.
You two are the inspiration to my world. I pray you will have great success as you navigate life's challenges with courage and an open heart.

To the folks who shaped my thinking—Mom and Dad.
Your nuggets of wisdom on forgiveness and grace echo through my life. Thank you for the sacrifice to lead me on the path I should go.

And to all the amazing people I've crossed paths with— friends, mentors, and fellow pioneers.
Your stories, challenges, and triumphs have fueled the narrative of my story. This book is dedicated to each of you who have demonstrated resilience and taught me the profound lessons of forgiveness.

Blessings on our shared journey

CONTENTS

REVIEW

by Rev. Chris Boeckel

R OB COBURN HAS NAILED IT. *UnCaught: A Practical Guide to Escaping the Trap of Offense* is a masterful piece written so practically as it unravels the complex mystery of offense. As I read page after page, I began to process different conflicts and offenses throughout my lifetime and guess what? I found some offenses that were not reconciled one hundred percent. I thought extending grace and sprinkling some forgiveness on top was sufficient. But as I read the words in this book, I realized my "Bear" (offense) was being poked.

Rob describes the trap, what offense is, understanding different types of offense, the result of offense, finding offense, forgiving offense, and being made whole. As my "Bear" was poked, I realized I had a couple types of offense I was entertaining. Rob helped me not only reveal these offenses, but also reconcile them. As my personal journey was unfolding, I realized the offenses I held on to actually hindered God's blessings fully in my life.

This book is a practical tool that *every* Christian of every denomination should have at ready to renew our minds (Romans 12:2) and live out Psalm 119:165—"Great peace have they which love thy law and NOTHING shall offend them." I am excited to share this book with our leadership team at Orchard Park Living Water Church and leave copies with everyone that decides to follow Jesus.

Living unoffended is how we were created to live.

FOREWORD

by Tommy Reid

As I OPENED THE PACKAGE containing this manuscript, the title literally leaped off the page to me. My heart seemed to skip a beat as I read the words *Escaping the Trap of Offense*. After spending over sixty years in the pulpit ministry and speaking to thousands of people, I immediately thought, "This is the book that had to be written."

Our culture today is driven by a pandemic of offense. Many lives have been shaped by an offense received through the life of a parent, a sibling, a child, a neighbor, a church member, or a close friend. Perhaps we have even been offended by an author of a book we recently read. We have all had offenses, and sometimes our personality has been forever altered by an offense growing in our heart. Not only has our life been altered, but our personal future of a truly productive life has been severely changed, altered, or destroyed by someone saying or doing something that offended us.

As I opened the manuscript, I thought to myself, "Thank God someone was brave enough to write this for our contemporary world." My mind raced over my long history of ministry, and I thought of so many born with great gifts who never reached their goals because of something someone did to offend them. As I read through the pages, my mind further thought of individuals who would have benefited from reading this book earlier in life. And I thought about how different life would have been if that friend of mine had not suffered that offense.

Another thought came to mind, and I wondered if perhaps some of the church's major problems, and even our world's problems, began when someone who was young and impressionable was offended. That offense began to dictate the future of their thinking and shaped their performance for the rest of their life. And the world never discovered that individual's gifts because an offense had destroyed their effectiveness in life.

Then, I thought about the consequences of harboring an offense as a minister of the Gospel. If that friend of mine had not been offended when they were very young, would it be possible that the world could have been changed had my friend not experienced that offense? Is it possible that the world has never been evangelized, great churches have never been built, or great corporations were never born simply because a potentially great leader was offended when they were very young? That offense in their childhood altered their personality so much that they never accomplished the work God assigned to them.

So, with those thoughts in mind, I carefully read each chapter. My mind was filled with many questions as I read the chapter titles. Some of the chapter titles caused strong emotions to fill my soul and challenge me. As I looked at titles like "What is an Offense" or the amazing chapter entitled "Offended at God," I felt a sledge hammer hit my brain telling me how important this book was to our society today. Other chapter titles disturbed me at first, but I knew the titles were true even though they contained statements that initially offended me. The very title of this book almost "haunted" me. Offense will come to all of us. I assure you it will come. What are we to do when it comes?

With these memories in mind, I invite you to take a journey with me as we read the words of this author. Perhaps they will cause you to think. Perhaps they will bring conviction to your life. Perhaps they will even cause you to repent. However, I firmly believe that, as you read this book, you will hear from God. Truth sometimes hurts, sometimes convicts, sometimes gives joy, sometimes brings us to repentance.

Read these pages with an open mind and a submissive spirit. If you do, I know that the Holy Spirit will speak to you. Most of all, I pray that the Lord will speak with you. And when God speaks, please listen; you may discover God and His voice in a way you have never heard it before. Then, get prepared to find God's purpose for your life and…

GO CHANGE YOUR WORLD!

INTRODUCTION

Have you ever wondered why it seems like you are stuck in life? Or why the church is not growing by leaps and bounds? The simple answer is offense.

Offense is defined as "the state of being insulted or morally challenged; the act of displeasing or affronting; something that outrages the moral or physical senses" (Merriam-Webster). The word *offense* is used to define the root of our word *scandal*. We can all agree that a scandal is something serious, so if offense is used in its definition, an offense is serious business as well.

Too many people, both church members and non-members, are carrying around offenses. These offenses alter lives to the point that people miss out on the abundant blessings God planned for them.

In 2022, I preached a sermon series on offense in our life. What I learned personally and what I taught my congregation altered the trajectory of our church. That sounds like a bold statement, but it is actually an understatement of reality. By the third week, I was receiving non-stop phone calls with invitations to breakfast and lunch because people wanted to talk. Every person I talked with made a similar statement: "There's something in my life that is keeping me from all that God has for me, and I want rid of it. I need to get rid of it. I need help." And we worked through the situation together, figuring out what went wrong and what needed to be done to move forward and receive all that God had for them.

The rest of this book contains those sermons that radically changed the lives of people as they dealt with the offenses in their lives. I hope that throughout these pages you find the abundance God has for you when you live a life free of offense. Don't be surprised if God wrecks your life, in a good way, as you read. We are going to take those broken pieces and put them back together again to make you better and stronger than you were before.

1

THE TRAP

WE ALL KNOW A MOUSE trap is harmless when it is not set. A mouse could crawl over the top of the trap, and it would not go off. We could walk around all day with a trap in our pocket, and it would not hurt us. However, as soon as the trap is set, it becomes activated and deadly.

The mouse smells the scent of cheese floating in the air and decides to investigate. It wanders close to the trap, sees the cheese, and wants a nibble. The mouse puts its paws on the trap, leans forward to taste the delicious cheese, and WHAM! The trap stick falls, the bar snaps forward, and the mouse's life is over.

The same is true of offense. Until we pick up an offense and own it, the offense is harmless because the trap isn't set. Once we pick up the offense, the cheese is on the trap. The offense becomes the trap stick, and the trap is set, activated, and triggered for something bad to happen in our life.

But think about this—the trap stick isn't what kills the mouse, right? And the cheese doesn't kill either. Only the bar snaps the mouse's neck and kills him. When we walk around offended, the offense (the trap stick) is simply part of the trigger. The actual offense itself does not kill us. It is the bitterness. It is the unforgiveness. It is the disease and sickness that invades when we allow an offense toward our spouse or pastor or boss to set the trap. All those emotions and internal thoughts triggered by the offense are what kill us.

If you have ever set a mouse trap in your house or garage, you are familiar with the commotion that happens when the trap goes off. You hear the loud snap of the trap, followed by some shuffling noises and silence. And then you think "Yes! I got one!" You might even shout and celebrate, depending on how pesky the mouse was. Our enemy, Satan, is watching the church and waiting to hear the snap of offense. He knows that, if he traps just one believer, the destiny of that person and the damage they were supposed to inflict on His kingdom will no longer happen.

So, how do we avoid the trap? We have to know and understand four things:

1. What an offense is;
2. What to do when we smell the cheese;
3. How to defend against the bar snapping down; and
4. How to process and restore offenses.

When we face the temptation of offense and smell the cheese on the trap, we have two choices—walk away or pick up the cheese to take a nibble. If we choose to pick up the cheese, we choose death. If we choose to walk way, we choose life. Yes, offense is that serious.

2

WHAT IS OFFENSE?

"Great peace have they which love thy law,
and nothing shall offend them" (Psalm 119:165, KJV).

HAVE YOU EVER LOOKED BACK on a conversation or situation and thought, "I don't know where that went wrong, but so-and-so shouldn't have reacted that way"? You scratched your head in the moment, but eventually, you forgot about what happened. Maybe, in the aftermath of the situation, your friendship with that person fractured and you never understood why. And then days, weeks, or even years later, the other person brings up what happened that day. Turns out, that person dwelled on the conversation or situation to the point of picking up an offense. While the whole situation was minor to you, it significantly impacted the other person's life even though you never meant your words or actions how that person interpreted them.

In the Introduction to this book, *offense* is defined as "the state of being insulted or morally challenged." Human nature is to react to an insult. If someone calls us a name, our feelings are hurt and we nurse our wounds. Sometimes we let their ugly words get under our skin and change how we view ourselves.

Other times, we let the insult roll off us like water off a duck's back. The insult does not bother us, and we continue with life as if nothing happened. When we let our feelings be hurt and we nurse our wounds, we're in the process of picking up an offense.

After I started teaching my congregation about offense, my phone rang off the hook every day. As I talked with people (and put on a few pounds thanks to all the great meals), the pieces of the puzzle started falling into place and I realized three truths about offense:

1. No one is exempt from being offended or at least having the temptation to be offended. It does not matter who you are—you will be tempted by offense at some point. Offense is an everyday part of our world, our churches, and our relationships. Even Jesus was tempted by offense when He walked on this earth. Scripture tells us that Jesus was tempted as we are yet without sin. If He had given in to the temptation and picked up an offense, we would have seen His life without fruit, without miracles, and without healing.

2. No one can offend us. Someone can do something offensive, but for it to offend us, we have to pick that offense up and own it. If you are offended, it is not because of the other person. It is because you picked up that offense, nursed it, and convinced yourself that you were right. What happens when we pick up an offense and nurse it? We lose the blessings God has for us. We watch the other person receive blessings and then we get more offended because the person who offended us is blessed. It is a vicious cycle, and we'll talk about how to break the cycle in later chapters.

3. All offenses can be sorted into one of three categories— imaginary, accidental, and purposeful. (If you are not sure which category an offense in your life falls into, don't worry because you will have a good idea by the end of this book.)

- **Imaginary offenses** do not actually happen. Someone takes a piece of information, adds it to another thought, decides they don't like an action, and as a result, creates an offense. No one actually did anything to the person to cause the offense. They fabricated the offense in their mind.
- **Accidental offenses** happen when words and actions are misinterpreted. We have all said things that are taken out of context and misconstrued. We did not mean the words how someone heard them, but their interpretation led to an offense.
- **Purposeful offenses** are actual, intentional offenses. The person meant to offend someone else. They knowingly said hurtful words or physically did something to offend.

Throughout this book, we'll take a deep dive into each of these truths using the Bible as our base. Scripture is loaded with stories of two kinds of people—those who chose to ignore the temptation of offense and those who chose to pick up an offense. During my study of Bible stories connected to offense, I discovered a direct correlation between offense and productivity in the kingdom. The people who gave in to the temptation, picked up an offense, and carried it became barren or failed to bear fruit in God's kingdom—exactly what Satan wants.

Carrying around an offense in life is serious. Luke 17 says, "It is impossible that no offenses should come, but woe to him through whom they do come! It would be better for him if a millstone were hung around His neck, and he were thrown into the sea, than that he should offend one of these little ones." Whoa. Offense is so serious that Jesus told His disciples—and I'm not going to speak lightly here—a person is better off drowning with a concrete block tied around His neck than being the source of an offense and spreading that offense to others, especially to less mature Christians.

Today, our churches are filled with non-productive, fruit-less people all because we have offenses tied around our neck. We have to do better. We have to gain the maturity to stand up and say "no" when someone offends us or tries to disperse an offense to us. The enemy (Satan) is never going to stop trying to offend us. He is going to attempt to offend us before we are saved. He is going to do it after we are saved. He is going to do it before we are healed, and he is going to do it after we are healed. No one is exempt from the temptation of being offended. The enemy is out to derail us through offense every single day. And sadly, many of us fall into His trap.

3

UNDERSTANDING TYPES OF OFFENSE

I F YOU ARE LIKE ME and have lived a few years of life, you have experienced offense or the temptation to be offended. It's easy for me to tell you to "get rid of offense in your life," but how applicable is that statement? How do we identify offense and make sure we can defend against the temptation?

One of the truths I realized as I studied offense in the Bible and talked to people is that all offenses can be sorted into one of three categories—imaginary, accidental, and purposeful. And sadly, all Christians have experienced at least one of these types of offense. The key to getting rid of offense is being able to identify which type of offense you are dealing with. Once you know the type, you will know how to process the offense and what steps to take to remove the offense from your life.

The first category—imaginary—is huge. This type of offense happens all the time. People get bent out of shape over the simplest things and sometimes over things that never happened. The event did not happen to the person, and it did not happen about the person, yet they are offended. When you sit down and ask for details about what happened, they say, "I don't know. I'm just offended over that." I call this type of offense an imaginary offense because the offense isn't real. They literally made the offense up. It might be based on reality, but the person cannot tie the offense to one specific situation. They simply feel like the offense happened, and their brain does stupid stuff to convince them the offense is reality and it really did happen.

First Samuel 18 gives us the perfect example of an imaginary offense. Saul is king, and he makes David a leader in the army as they battle the Philistines. Together, Saul and David go to battle and return home. They're greeted by the people in the streets singing "Saul has slain His thousands, and David His ten thousands." And Saul is offended.

David does not actually do anything to offend Saul, yet Saul sees David as a threat. David simply does the right things and what God tells him. He shows up in the right places. As a result, the success David experiences offends Saul—even though David's success means Saul's kingdom is now a powerhouse against the Philistines.

I imagine a few of you are saying, "But I can see why Saul would be offended at David's success. The people liked David better and praised him more than Saul, their king and leader." Okay, I understand where you are coming from. But did Saul have the right to be offended just because people were praising David? Did David commit an offense against Saul? No, Saul imagined the offense between the two of them. Over time, the relationship between Saul and David deteriorated because of Saul's imaginary offense. And that imaginary offense cost Saul everything, including His family members and His throne.

Let's look at another example of imaginary offenses. In the middle of preaching this series on offense, I had the opportunity to travel to Buffalo, New York, for an event. During my time there, I did some soul-searching just to get my own soul clear. As a pastor ministering to a couple hundred people, I carry a lot of stuff around, some of which I don't even know I am carrying at times. I decided to dump some of that stuff off, and in that process, I uncovered some imaginary offenses. Yes, you read that right—I was in the middle of preaching a series on offense and discovered I had imaginary offenses in my life. I had thought something about a person or situation, but my thought was wrong. And those thoughts clogged up the productivity in my life. So what did I do? I got my heart right. I forgave myself, and then I forgave the people involved in every situation where I had an imaginary offense. And I can honestly say that after I got my heart right, I was a different person.

While preaching the series on offense in my church, I shared meals with a lot of people. One meal conversation comes to mind whenever I think about imaginary offenses. I'm going to call this person John, but that's not the person's real name. We were discussing offense, and John told me he was offended at Sam (again, not a real name). As John described what happened, I couldn't help but ask, "How can you be offended at Sam? Do you know him well?" I was pretty sure they were barely acquaintances. They routinely sat on opposite sides of the auditorium during services, and I couldn't recall ever seeing them interact with each other beyond saying hello. John replied to my question with "Well, I was around Sam and I heard what he did. Now I'm offended." Did Sam do something offensive? No. John perceived it as offensive and created an imaginary offense.

Think about this—if the enemy (Satan) can use our imaginations to find offenses that do not really exist and as a result stop us from being productive in the kingdom, how important is it for us to change our imaginations? We need to imagine the things God wants us to and put that power to good use. If you discover you have imaginary offenses in your life, search your soul. Do not let your imagination win. Ask God to show you the situations where you need to seek forgiveness. (We'll explore the process of overcoming offense in-depth in later chapters.)

The second category of offense—accidental—is probably the biggest, but not the most potent. Have you ever done something by accident and someone got offended? I'm a pastor, and I stand in front of hundreds of people every week. Sometimes I say things accidentally or in ways that can be interpreted differently. Someone takes what I said the wrong way and gets offended by it. I did not mean to offend that person, but they got offended. That offense is accidental or unintentional.

Go back to the simple example at the beginning of Chapter Two. You may not have intentionally tried to offend the other person. You may have had no clue you even offended them. But yet, that person was bound for days, weeks, or years over that offense. And when we are bound by these accidental offenses, we allow emotions—bitterness, frustration, anger—to take over and hang like weights around our neck. These offenses destroy our relationships and ruin our marriages when we fail to confront them and deal with them biblically. We assume the other person meant to offend us, we allow our emotions to derail us, and we fail to talk about the offense. When a person says something or does something that offends us and we don't talk to that person, we have no way of knowing if the person really meant to offend us. Before long, there's a wall in the relationship, and the wall continues to grow higher and higher. We must be bold enough to do what the Bible says—handle the offense, tear down the wall, and get back to normal.

Satan loves to use accidental and imaginary offenses to keep the church in turmoil and constantly stirred up. (I'm sure you have heard of church politics and all the crazy stuff that can happen in a church.) And when the church is in turmoil, the church is stuck and not building God's kingdom. What we need to do is call Satan out and say, "Listen, I'm not going to be offended. I love God and I love His Word." We must stand firm on Psalm 119:165—"Great peace have they which love thy law, and nothing shall offend them."

The third category of offense is a purposeful offense when a person intentionally tries to offend someone else through words or actions. These are the offenses that hurt the most. Premeditated crimes and all forms of abuse fall under this category, and so do those words you know you should not say because they will hurt the other person, but you say them anyway.

Just like the other types of offense, a purposeful offense can destroy relationships. However, this type of offense differs because it is the hardest offense to deal with. The pain from a purposeful offense runs deep.

When an offender is confronted, most of the time they deny the purposeful offense and fail to acknowledge the offense even occurred. And the offender will probably never apologize to the person they offended. On the flip side, when someone approaches me about an accidental offense I caused, I can apologize even though I was clueless about offending the person. I learn from the situation, and the person I offended experiences healing because I apologized.

Along with a lack of forgiveness and subsequent healing, a purposeful offense is painful because the offender will not change, and that makes the weight and pain of this type of offense harder to carry. If we are the person who was offended, our only option is to pray for the offender, forgive them, and minister to them the best we can. During that process, the Holy Spirit may change their heart, but honestly, He will probably change our hearts and help us walk in forgiveness.

In the Bible, the best example of a purposeful offense happened to Jesus when Judas betrayed Him. Judas walked with Jesus and was His financial guy. Judas sat at the table, and Jesus served him. And then, in exchange for thirty pieces of silver, Judas betrayed Jesus and led the soldiers directly to Him in the garden. Judas knew what he was doing that night. He did it on purpose and all for some money. Jesus had every human right to be offended at Judas, but He was not. (And we'll go deeper into why Jesus was not offended in a later chapter.)

When we are on the receiving end of a purposeful offense, what happens when we allow that offense to fester in our hearts?

We will look at these points in-depth in the next two chapters, but in a nutshell:

1. We think about the offense.
2. We feed the emotions (bitterness, anger, etc.) created by the offense.
3. Eventually, the offense destroys a part of our life.
4. Satan uses the offense to derail us from what God has for us.
5. And, as a result, we fail to experience the blessings and fruitfulness God wants for us.

CASE STUDY #1

THE MAN BY THE POOL

NOW THAT WE KNOW THE three categories of offense, let's look at John 5 and the story of Jesus walking by the pool. As you read the verses, keep your antenna up for places where an offense could happen.

> Now there is in Jerusalem by the Sheep Gate a pool, which is called in Hebrew, Bethesda, having five porches. In these lay a great multitude of sick people, blind, lame, paralyzed, waiting for the moving of the water. For an angel went down at a certain time into the pool and stirred up the water; then whoever stepped in first, after the stirring of the water, was made well of whatever disease he had. Now a certain man was there who had an infirmity thirty-eight years.
>
> When Jesus saw him lying there, and knew that he already had been in that condition a long time, He said to him, "Do you want to be made well?"
>
> The sick man answered Him, "Sir, I have no man to put me into the pool when the water is stirred up, but while I am coming, another steps down before me."
>
> Jesus said to him, "Rise, take up your bed and walk."
>
> And immediately the man was made well, took up His bed, and walked. (vv. 2–9)

Let's put that story into today's perspective and figure out where the offenses could have occurred.

Jesus and His disciples are walking around town and hear the noise of a crowd. They follow the sound and discover a crowd gathered around the fountain in the town square. Jesus and His disciples stand on the edge of the crowd and watch as the water is stirred and the crowd surges forward. Some people are climbing in the fountain; others have their cell phones out ready to video the miraculous healings.

Jesus notices a man sitting in a wheelchair on a nearby porch just watching the crowd. The man does not try to wheel His chair down the porch ramp to possibly be the first to enter the fountain waters. No, he just stays on the porch. Jesus, knowing the man had been sick for almost forty years, walks up to him and asks if he wants to be healed.

Now, stop and think for a second. How many people did that man watch be healed over the years? Every day, people got in the water, got out, got in, got out—hundreds of people healed each year. Yet, the man is still there watching. And he is still sick.

How easy would it be to get offended in this man's situation? At some point over the years, he could've picked up an offense, nursed it, and carried it around. He could've become bitter. He watched all those people be healed, yet he was still stuck in His wheelchair. Right there is His first opportunity for offense.

Go back to the question Jesus asked him—"Do you want to be healed?" The man had been in a wheelchair for thirty-eight years and then a stranger walks up and asks if he wants to be healed. Would we be offended by a question like that with an obvious answer? Who wouldn't want to be healed? And that's the second opportunity for offense.

Instead of being offended, the man replies, "No one else will help me." This man had been waiting for years and years for healing. He is at the fountain waiting. Yet, none of His friends or even a stranger will help him into the water. In fact, people are so self-centered and focused on their own desire for healing that they push him out of the way and jump in front of him. When we are constantly pushed to the side, it is easy to become offended and hurt. That's strike number three in this story.

Even with three opportunities for offense, the man is told to "Rise, take up your bed, and walk." If this man had picked up even one of those offenses and allowed bitterness at God to take root, he likely never would have received the blessing of being healed. If we are offended at Jesus, we do not get up and walk away completely healed. We have to manage our life so we don't get offended at man and we don't get offended at God.

"Wait, Pastor Rob, did you just say that we can be offended at God?" Yes. Have you ever attended a church service where the Holy Spirit is moving? People are responding; they're being touched by the Spirit, but you are standing there saying, "Why not me? Why not me?" You walk out after the service and think, "Hmmm. Maybe I shouldn't go to the next service because I didn't get _____ at that one." You are offended at God.

If you are offended with God, it is your problem. It is your thoughts. It is your situational perspective. It is not God, because God isn't capable of hurting us. God wants to help, not hurt. He's looking down from heaven saying, "I want people and a church that is so in love with me and my Word that they cannot get offended and they can be so productive in my kingdom that they will bring heaven to earth every single day."

God wants to raise up an army of people who are not offended at Him. When we are offended at Him, we cannot be productive. I believe that the global church as a whole has been offended at God for some crazy things. Some preacher said something twenty years ago or something happened, and we walked away from God. Someone did not get healed the first time when the church prayed for them, and we walked away from God. The pastor did something stupid, and we walked away. Maybe those things are imaginary. Maybe they're accidental. Either way,

Christians are human, and we simply need to grow up and deal with the offenses we encounter on a daily basis.

Let's go back to the man in John 5. Jesus tells him to pick up His bed and walk, so he does. Within minutes, another opportunity for offense presents itself. The Jews said, "It is the Sabbath. It is not lawful for you to carry your bed." The man just went through three opportunities to be offended at God, but he did not give in to the temptation of offense. As soon as he is healed, the religious people come after him and tell him to not carry His bed. How easy would it have been for the man to get offended at the religious people? He had been sick for years and years and finally experienced healing, and now the religious people are telling him he is breaking the law. Instead of picking up an offense, he smiled and told them he had been healed and then went on His way.

4

PICKING UP OFFENSE

Nurse, Rehearse, Disperse

PART OF THE DEFINITION OF *offense* is "the state of being insulted or morally challenged." For us to be insulted, we have to take what the other person said or did and own it. We have to internalize it and make it about us. An insult is only an insult when we let it be one. Being degraded or called a dirty word hurts only if we let it. Same thing for an offense. An offense isn't something a person actually does to us. Their actions or words might be offensive, but actions or words offend us *only* when we pick up the offense and make it ours.

Do you remember the childhood saying "Sticks and stones may hurt my bones, but words can never hurt me"? We all know words can hurt, but the moral of that saying is the words only hurt us if we let them. Again, the same thing for an offense. It is only an offense if we let it be offensive.

When someone says something offensive to us, we pick up the offense and start to nurse it and treat it with care. Think about the mouse trap illustration. We gingerly carry a set trap. We do not want the trap stick to fall and the bar to snap down, so we make sure we have two hands on the trap as we move it. Offenses are the same as the mouse trap. We are very careful with an offense when it first happens. We nurse it and say, "Oooh, I don't want this to go off because it could really hurt me." We keep the offense in check and have two hands on it at all times. But then after we move the trap around enough, we start to think maybe we can carry it with one hand and still be okay.

The process of nursing or carefully treating an offense feels good. We soothe our wounds while thinking about the offense; however, sometimes we think about the offense so much that it becomes boring. So what do we do after we nurse it for a little bit? We rehearse it. We start to think about it all the time. It consumes us and distracts us from daily life. Maybe we even dream about it. We rehearse, rehearse, and rehearse just like we are preparing for a performance. We turn over the offense so much in our mind that we fully believe our version of the offense. (This rehearsing stage is where a lot of imaginary and accidental offenses are blown out of proportion.)

What I have discovered is that when we rehearse an offense, the offense becomes more intense because now the enemy is in our mind with that offense. Sometimes we rehearse the offense so much that we don't even remember what happened in reality. All we know is that we are comfortable with the rehearsed offense. We walk around with it. We bounce it around. We do whatever we want with the offense, and we don't think it will hurt us.

After we nurse and rehearse the offense enough, we disperse it. We do not warn people when we are about to disperse an offense either. No, we just talk and tell the story. "Can you believe so-and-so did this thing to me? I can't believe it. They are so..."

The problem with dispersing the story is the poison of the offense affects other people. The person listening to our story now carries the same offense around that we are carrying.

Dispersing an offense is the step that the Lord in Luke 17 commands us to never engage in—"It is impossible that no offenses should come, but woe to him through whom they do come!" If you cause an offense or if you disperse an offense, you are in violation of Luke 17. Unfortunately, the culture in our world today disperses offenses every day without warning. Here is how simple it is:

> One of your church friends stops by your house Sunday afternoon. The first words out of her mouth are "The pastor is such an idiot." She just handed an offense to you without warning. You were not in church that morning because your toddler was sick, so you have no idea what she is talking about. You never heard what the pastor said. You never saw the look on the pastor's face. You never heard the songs that were sung that morning. Your mind starts to think about what your friend said and how she described what happened. Before long, if you are not careful, you start to question whether the pastor is an idiot like your friend said. You have now picked up and owned someone else's offense.

When our offense is dispersed to someone else, we feel good about it. It is out of our hands because we passed it to someone else, right? Sadly, that's not how it works. We are liable for wherever that offense goes once we disperse it. It may stay with the person we dispersed it to or that person may spread the offense. If they spread the offense, we are responsible for whoever dies with the offense. I know that sounds heavy, but you have to understand the weight of offense. If I handed you an offense right now, you would follow the natural human pattern for dealing with offense—nurse, rehearse, and disperse. The problem is I'm responsible for what you disperse because I gave you the offense.

If we are perpetuating offense, we have to restore all of it. If I said something about someone to someone else, and they repeated it to somebody, I am responsible because I started the offense. I have to restore all those relationships all the way down the line. Let's take a bird's eye view of how that looks:

Matt and Amy attend the wedding of Matt's coworker. At the reception, Matt is talking with five of His buddies. They're laughing and joking around, and before long, Matt tells an awesome story and disperses an offense in the process. His five buddies, maybe without realizing they're dispersing an offense, tell Matt's story to someone else at the reception. Now ten people have heard Matt's offense. By the end of the next week, those ten people each tell ten others. That group of one hundred tells more people, and by the end of the month, over one thousand people have heard Matt's story containing the offense.

Because Matt was the one who dispersed the offense, he is responsible in the kingdom of heaven for the restoration of all those people. Why? Because the restoration is as broad as the offense every time. When someone comes to you with an offense, do you want to be in that chain of apologizing and restoring everything? I know I don't want to, and I don't think you do either. If you realize you have been offended and you have spread offense, go fix it now. Before the end of the day, apologize. If the person you need to apologize to is no longer alive, fix it in your heart between you and God.

"Well, that's all fine, Pastor Rob, but how do I avoid being in the position to disperse an offense?" We'll talk more about how to defend against offense in a later chapter, but for now, here is the short version. Instead of taking an offense, coddling it for a while, getting comfortable with it because you've played with it so much, and then dispersing it, stop and deploy the defense God gave us in Psalm 119:165—"Great peace have they which love thy law, and nothing shall offend them."

When that offense starts brewing in your mind or that friend tries to hand you an offense without warning, say, "No, no, no. Not for me." Hand the offense back. The Bible tells us this works if we love the law. However, here's the lowdown— not many mature people can hand an offense back. Very few can refuse an offense. Those who can will say "I don't want that because you know what? When I take that offense, we both die. The trap stick falls, and the bar clamps down."

The longer we accept offense in our individual lives, the more offended the world becomes. We have an offended church, offended leaders, offended pastors, offended business people, offended politicians, and the list could go on. Everyone is offended. Why do we have this problem? Is it because all these people experienced the offense? Not necessarily. They're offended because people nursed an offense, rehearsed it, and then dispersed it to them. What used to be a little thing now becomes a big thing because we lack the maturity to say we are not picking up the offense and helping carry it. As a result, the fruitfulness of the church as a whole is damaged. Sometimes entire ministries become fruit-less. And it is all because offense was nursed, rehearsed, and dispersed. We have to raise our maturity level, say no, and refuse offense.

5

OFFENDED AT GOD

IF YOU HAVE READ THIS far, you probably realize two things:- first, you can have a lot of offenses with man, and second, being offended is a big deal. What we fail to understand sometimes is we carry offenses toward God too. We may not even understand the offenses, but a lot of them go back to the Old Testament law.

When God gave Moses the law, the wrath of heaven was revealed, curses came from it, and punishment came as well. But, at the same time, the law brought freedom. Curses and punishment are contradictory to something that offers freedom, so it is pretty easy to see where misunderstanding starts, right?

Deuteronomy 28:1–2 tells us:

> Now it shall come to pass, if you diligently obey the voice of the LORD your God, to observe carefully all His commandments which I command you today, that the LORD your God will set you high above all nations of the earth. And all these blessings shall come upon you and overtake you, because you obey the voice of the LORD your God:

The next twelve verses list a bunch of blessings for those who obey God. We read those first fourteen verses and think, "Man, if I love the Lord and obey all His commandments, all these blessings are mine. This is amazing!" Except we fail to continue reading the rest of the chapter.

Verse fifteen says, "But it shall come to pass, if you do not obey the voice of the Lord your God, to observe carefully all His commandments and His statutes which I command you today, that all these curses will come upon you and overtake you:"

The blessings can turn to curses when we fail to obey. Notice that the verse uses the word *all*—"do not...observe carefully all His commandments and His statutes." That means if we break one jot or tittle of that law—just a fraction about the size of the dot above the *j* in "jot"—the blessings disappear and curses take their place. Boy, talk about pressure for God's chosen people. Drive your chariot one mile per hour over the speed limit and your blessings leave. Forget which day of the week it is and scramble eggs for your kids' breakfast on the Sabbath, say goodbye to those blessings. While these are lighthearted examples, living under the Old Testament law was a lot of pressure.

Today, Christians carry the same pressure. We want God to move greatly and powerfully, but some of us are still bound by the Old Testament law. We believe God gave our spouse cancer to teach our family a lesson. Or we believe God took our mom to heaven as a punishment for something we did. Those beliefs are Old Testament law.

When we are bound by the law, we cannot step into the fullness of what God has for us and accept the New Testament grace. We meet Jesus, but we don't accept what He has paid for and the revelation of the cross. Our life does not change. Why? Either we failed to understand God's grace or we accepted Jesus with some Old Testament law attached.

The Bible says, "By their fruit, you shall know them." When our experience and our fruit fail to match up with Scripture, we have to go back to God and ask Him to change us. The first step in that change is recognizing that we are offended at God. Yes, I just said we can be offended at God.

Let's use the example of believing God uses sickness as a lesson to teach us something. What happens when we pray for healing and it doesn't come how we expect it? What happens when we learn the lesson God intended and no one is healed? The enemy rears His ugly head and lays out the temptation. He presents the opportunity for us to be offended. "God, we prayed, asking for healing, and the healing never came. You failed us." And we leave the church and put our Bible away on the shelf. We are living, knowing Jesus, but we have a foot stuck in the law. Before long, we lose our productivity in the kingdom and fail to produce fruit. Disease is not of God in any case. He is not that guy and that is not how God operates. He is a God of love and compassion, not a punisher.

What about the person who believes God took a loved one as punishment? Now, I grew up Baptist, and I always thought that it was my sin that worked the law (punishment) in my life. My mind equated committing a sin with subsequently encountering the law, so I understand the thought process that God uses punishment if we break the law. But that's not what Romans 4:15 says: "For if those who are of the law *are* heirs, faith is made void and the promise made of no effect, because the law brings about wrath; for where there is no law *there is* no transgression." My sin did not bring God's wrath. The law itself unleashes God's wrath on the world.

As I was studying the idea of being offended at God, I asked the Lord, "If the law is everything I think it is, why didn't Adam have the law? Why didn't Moses have it in the beginning? What about Noah and Enoch? Why didn't they have the law? Why did it take so long to put the law on the earth?"

God knew that when the law came, it would release His wrath, and His wrath was not and is not His heart for His people. He did not give us sickness or death to teach us a lesson. He did not give us those things to change who we are. He did not take our spouse or family member to teach us something because the family had a sinful past. The only reason He brought the law was because He had to, but then He brought Jesus.

"Christ has redeemed us from the curse of the law, having become a curse for us (for it is written, 'Cursed *is* everyone who hangs on a tree'), that the blessing of Abraham might come upon the Gentiles in Christ Jesus, that we might receive the promise of the Spirit through faith" (Galatians 3:13–14). Those verses are the revelation that unlocks us from the curse of the law. Christ redeemed us. Jesus paid it all. Even though Jesus did it all and we can claim it, if we do not actually receive what He did, our feet are still in the Old Testament law and our mind is bound. God did not want to pour out wrath, but He had to in order to have righteousness, and the cross was the final culmination of His wrath.

The most important questions you can ask yourself at this point are: Even if I know who Jesus is, am I offended at Him? Am I offended at God for something some religious person (pastor, teacher, deacon, church leader) told me a long time ago? Have I walked out of church? Maybe you slowly stopped attending and never thought about why. Over the years that I have been a pastor, I learned something—when people get offended at God, they don't come back inside the church. Why? Because it is hard to be in the presence of the person you are offended at.

Maybe you answered those questions in the last paragraph with a "No" and you are saying "Phew, I'm off the hook. I'm not offended at God." Not so fast. In my church, we have a discipleship process and the first three parts of that process are:

1. Reading your Bible every day,
2. Encountering the Holy Spirit, and
3. Building healthy relationships.

If you cannot make it past the first step of reading the Word every day, there's something between you and Jesus. If you do not want to be in the presence of the Lord, if you do not want to hear His voice, if you do not want Him to change you, examine your heart for an offense with God. Maybe that offense goes back twenty years; maybe it came from twenty minutes ago. How long you have been carrying and nursing that offense with God doesn't matter. You need to examine your heart, ask for forgiveness, and release the offense.

6

THE RESULT OF OFFENSE

Unfruitful and Barren

I'M GOING TO BE BLUNT—WHEN the trap of offense is sprung, bitterness and brokenness enter your life and you become dead in the kingdom. Did I just say that we die and don't get to go to heaven? No, not at all. What I mean by "you become dead" is offense causes us to become infertile, non-productive, non-fruit-bearing in God's kingdom. Another word for non-fruit-bearing is barren. Sadly, many Christians live barren lives and fail to be fruitful. This is contrary to God's plan. He did not call us to be barren or infertile; He told us to be fruitful and multiply—

> God created man in His own image; in the image of God he created him; male and female he created them. Then God blessed them, and God said to them, "Be fruitful and multiply; fill the earth and subdue it; have dominion over the fish of the sea, over the birds of the air, and over every living thing that moves on the earth." (Genesis 1:27–28)

When we hear the phrase "Be fruitful and multiply," we tend to focus on the "multiply." We hear about multiplying all the time in the natural and in the supernatural. (The word *multiply* is what young married couples love to gravitate toward.) Multiplication means to grow exponentially and is different from addition. If you are anything like me, you're happy when you look at your retirement portfolio and it has multiplied instead of just been added to. Genesis 1 tells us that if we are going to actually be fruitful, we need to multiply exponentially or grow and then take dominion over what He has given us.

Before we go further, let's take a step backward because we skipped over what happened before the multiplying. Look closely at Genesis 1:28. Before the phrase "be fruitful and multiply," there's a blessing—"God blessed them." Do you realize that we are blessed beyond measure? It may not seem like it at times, but we are. The simple fact that we wake up breathing every morning is a blessing. In fact, we are so blessed that we cannot even contain the blessings God has for us. No container on earth is big enough to hold what God has already spoken over us.

"But, Pastor Rob, I don't feel blessed."

If you are walking around not feeling blessed, it is not because of offense. Offense suppresses our ability to be fruitful, but it does not steal the blessings that come before the command to be fruitful. If you do not feel blessed, you are missing the boat because you are focused on what you can do for God when He has already done everything that you need Him to do for you. Stop focusing on what you can do and focus on the blessings of what God has already done for you.

After the blessing, the verse continues with the command to "be fruitful and multiply." How many people in America's churches skip over the first part—be fruitful? They immediately want to multiply because the Lord commanded them to, and that's great. But they fail to be fruitful. And if they aren't fruitful, what are they multiplying?

We already learned that, when we are in offense, we are spreading or dispersing offense to other people. So if we are spreading offense and allowing offense to rule our life, we are multiplying dysfunction (impaired or abnormal functioning). Today's world has a lot of dysfunctional relationships producing more dysfunction because we have failed to be fruitful and are busy multiplying offense.

If we follow the proper order given in Genesis and don't skip over being fruitful, the rest of the verse says we are to "fill the earth and subdue it; have dominion over the fish of the sea, over the birds of the air, and over every living thing that moves on the earth." If we are not fruitful, we cannot multiply good things. And if we cannot multiply good things, we cannot subdue the earth or have dominion over it. The Bible says that the heavens are the Lord's and the earth He has given to man, so we have His authority to have dominion.

We often say as Christians that the blessing of Abraham rests on us because we are the seed of His blessing. And that's true. However, there's one thing that Abraham did not have that we have access to—he did not have dominion. Think about that for a minute. We hold Abraham up to be this great guy, and he was. The problem is he walked in the promise of God, but he did not have the dominion of God. Abraham only had one piece of the puzzle. Jesus, on the other hand, walked in the promise of God and had dominion over the earth. So while it is good to talk about the Abrahamic covenant, we need to talk about the Jesus covenant. I want to be in the covenant where Jesus walks in the will of the Father and He walks in dominion on the earth. And if we are walking in the path of the Father and offenses come, what will the offenses do? If we let them attach to us, they will turn us away from the Father and we will lose dominion. If we cast the offense aside and say "No, not today," we will continue to bear fruit, multiply, and have dominion.

> And this I pray, that your love may abound still more and more in knowledge and all discernment, that you may approve the things that are excellent, that you may be sincere

and without offense till the day of Christ, being filled with the fruits of righteousness which are by Jesus Christ, to the glory and praise of God. (Philippians 1:9–11)

Let Apostle Paul's words sink in. What does he say the key to having a fruitful life is? Being without offense. We can be offended with our spouse. We can be offended with our church. We can be offended with the pastor. We can be offended with our workplace. We can be offended with our politicians. We can be offended with our government. We can be offended with other countries. We can be offended with people we have never even met and have only been told are bad. We can pick up any of those offenses, but Paul tells us that if we do, we will not be filled with the fruits of righteousness. We will be barren.

The ultimate goal of Satan is to distract us from the power we possess and the dominion we have within us. When we pick up an offense, it does not matter where we are or who offends us. Immediately, at that moment, the trap is set, and we become barren in our life. We no longer produce fruit until we deal with the offense. Satan wants our focus to be on the person who offended us so that we cannot walk in the fullness of who we really are. Offense limits our belief, and in turn, it limits our miracles and keeps us from our destiny.

When the enemy puts the idea in our mind of being offended at someone, the trap is there and waiting. We smell the cheese. Our focus shifts from what God put in us to everything around us, just like the mouse catches a whiff of the cheese and is no longer interested in building its nest. It wants the cheese and goes after the cheese.

CASE STUDY #2

REAL LIFE

In sharing the following scenario, I'm not being rude or trying to make light of the pain any survivor of abuse has endured. My heart weeps for survivors and the brokenness they live with. As Christians, our responsibility is to understand that purposeful, horrible offenses are really happening every day to people in our neighborhoods, work places, and churches. We have to learn how to confront these offenses and how to lead others in overcoming these life-altering offenses.

DURING MY YEARS OF MINISTRY, I have talked with individuals who have had heinous things done to them as children by close relatives—people children should be able to trust. As a result of what happened in their childhood, these victims have lived their lives bound to that place of abuse, nursing the purposeful offenses against them sometimes for decades.

Because these individuals are walking around carrying offenses and all their baggage, they have never been fruitful in God's kingdom. They have never had dominion over their life. Everything that comes at them takes advantage of them. Some end up addicted to drugs or alcohol; others battle eating disorders and dysfunctional relationships. They're broken and often do not see the way out of the pit the abuse threw them into. They have never handed anything over to God. Or if they have, they still hang on to a small sliver rather than release *all* the hurt, pain, anger, bitterness, and more to God. Life is seriously tough for these people.

The problem is they have welcomed not only the spirit of offense, but all that other stuff too. Their focus is on what happened in the past, not on what is happening in front of them. A misplaced focus is exactly what Satan wants so he can destroy individuals. He wants families fractured. His goal is our failure. When someone cannot see the everyday blessings because abuse has clouded their vision, Satan wins.

To overcome a serious, purposeful offense like abuse and step into a fruitful life, we must understand what the Bible tells us about God. He is the ultimate judge—"Vengeance is mine; I will repay, saith the Lord." That verse means we say to God:

> "I know you are the judge. You are the rightful judge and you are going to have vengeance. And if this is against me, I know that Satan is going to repay me. He has to repay me for what he took. He came in and stole some things in my life. But I don't want him to steal anymore. I'm going to hand the whole situation over to you, Lord, right now because you are a good judge and you are going to have vengeance. I don't have to worry about it anymore. Take this offense and all its dysfunction and cast it as far as the east is from the west."

And then watch and rejoice at the healing that flows abundantly from a heart free of offense. When all the hurt and brokenness from the past is released, the enemy who entered and wreaked havoc is stopped. We have the freedom to be fruitful and multiply.

If you are a survivor who is struggling with whatever someone did to you in the past, whether as a child or adult, ask God to help you understand two things:

1. When you offer forgiveness, you are not condoning that person for what they did. Forgiveness is not saying their actions were acceptable; it is saying "I'm releasing you from the debt you have caused upon my life. You have to answer for what you did, but I'm releasing you from it and placing it in the hands of a good judge. I'm going to live free and not allow Satan to rule over me any longer."

2. God is the ultimate judge. Vengeance is His. That person who committed those acts against you may be living in hell on earth. Their life may look fine on the outside, but they are tortured on the inside. The Bible promises they will be held accountable to God one day. Stand on that promise, and let God have His vengeance.

CASE STUDY #3

DAVID AND MICHAL

2 Samuel 6

STRICT RULES IN BIBLE TIMES governed how the Ark of God was to be transported and how and when it could be touched. In Second Samuel 6, David and His men are moving the ark from one location to another. During the journey, the oxen pulling the cart with the ark stumble, and a man by the name of Uzzah reaches out to steady the ark. As soon as Uzzah touches the cart, God strikes him dead.

> And David became angry because of the LORD's outbreak against Uzzah; ... David was afraid of the LORD that day; and he said, "How can the ark of the LORD come to me?" So David would not move the ark of the LORD with him into the City of David; but David took it aside into the house of Obed-Edom the Gittite. The ark of the LORD remained in the house of Obed-Edom the Gittite three months. And the LORD blessed Obed-Edom and all His household.

When Uzzah died, David got angry, or in other words, he picked up an offense at God. One of the men whom David told to drive the cart carrying the ark did not do His job the right way, and now the man is dead. When somebody is doing something we tell them to do and they are killed or injured in the process, there's an immediate weight, a burden, that overtakes our life.

After Uzzah's death, David finds himself in a predicament. He is understandably upset and carrying the weight of Uzzah's death. Then, over the next few weeks, he has to process the fact that Obed-Edom, the guy he left the ark with, is being blessed. Talk about a double whammy. First, Uzzah dies, and now other people are blessed—but David isn't. Somehow when we are offended and we see someone being blessed, we get more offended. Mentally and emotionally, the offense takes a toll on us.

David takes a few months to process and deal with the situation, and finally, one day, he says, "Wait a minute. I cannot go back and have a deeper pity party and be more offended. I have to change something."

How did David reach that realization? He had a heart after God's and kept God on the throne of His heart. Experience taught David that he needed to dig deep and evaluate the situation. He knew something in His life was messed up and he had to fix it. He knew he had to change himself, not others around him.

Next, David dealt with the problem, and in verse twelve, it says that he went with gladness to retrieve the ark. David owned up to His mistake of getting mad at God and knew he needed the presence of God back in His life. And when the presence of God came back, "David danced before the Lord with all His might; and David was wearing a linen ephod. So David and all the house of Israel brought up the ark of the Lord with shouting and with the sound of the trumpet" (verses 14–15).

David released the offense, and joy overcame him. I imagine David said something like "Wow! This is amazing! I'm so happy. I'm bringing the presence of God back into my life. I'm going to dance. I'm going to shout praises to God." He was free of the offense and had restored His relationship with God. But there's turmoil coming.

David, full of joy, hosted a party all along His journey home as His men carried the ark to the City of David. When they entered the city gates, verse sixteen tells us that "Michal, Saul's daughter, looked through a window and saw King David leaping and whirling before the LORD; and she despised him in her heart." Whoa. Michal is David's wife, and she is not happy with her husband. "Despised" is a strong word, making it obvious she is offended at David for dancing in the streets.

David, not knowing His wife is offended, continues partying, offers burnt offerings, and then blesses the people. He hands out bread, meat, and cakes of raisins to all the people before going home to bless His own household. If David had still been bound up in offense, I doubt he would be blessing people and feeding them healthy food.

Imagine the next scene when David gets home. Full of joy and happiness because the weight of offense (Uzzah's death) was lifted off His shoulders, David enters the palace gates. His wife greets him and says, "'How glorious was the king of Israel today, uncovering himself today in the eyes of the maids of His servants, as one of the base fellows shamelessly uncovers himself!'" (verse 20). Can you hear her tone of voice and the sarcasm dripping from her words?

The Bible does not tell us how much time passed between when Michal saw David through the window and when David arrived home. All we know is it was long enough for Michal to nurse and rehearse the offense and allow the enemy to take over her mind.

> So David said to Michal, "It was before the LORD, who chose me instead of your father and all His house, to appoint me ruler over the people of the LORD, over Israel. Therefore I will play music before the LORD. And I will be even more

undignified than this, and will be humble in my own sight. But as for the maidservants of whom you have spoken, by them I will be held in honor." Therefore Michal the daughter of Saul had no children to the day of her death. (vv. 21–23)

Did you catch that last sentence? Because Michal was offended at David for dancing in the streets, she was barren for the rest of her life. Honestly, I feel like Michal sort of got a bad deal. She paid a high price for being offended at David. The Bible does not tell us if offense was a pattern for her, but one offense was serious enough that it resulted in the loss of her fertility.

For us, Michal's story means we cannot have a fruitful life, a fruitful marriage, a fruitful business, or a fruitful anything if we are offended. As long as we carry an offense, our life will always be barren and lack fruit.

Thankfully, we have a freedom in Jesus today that Michal couldn't have. If you are barren in your walk with Jesus, your ministry, or your marriage, or if life is just rough, it can all change because Jesus took the iniquity of the cross on himself. We are covered under a new covenant. We receive from Jesus the forgiveness of everything He paid for on the cross. If we are not bearing fruit today because of offense, we can bear fruit tomorrow as long as we deal with the offense.

What can we learn from David and Michal?

- **Offense costs us.** It does not matter where we are or who offends us. Immediately, when we pick up that offense, we become barren in our life. Through the years, people with offense have experienced disease and sickness, unhappiness, poverty, and so much more. How much are you willing to pay for coddling an offense?
- **It is okay to change.** If we own up to making a mistake, we can change it. If we do not own up to a mistake, we cannot change it. David knew he had made the mistake of getting mad at God. He was bound up in offense, but

he realized he was wrong and needed the presence of God in His life. When we are offended at God or anyone else, the presence of God is not with us.

- **Emerge from offense with gladness.** David made things right with God and came out of the offense laughing and dancing. He was happy and had a deeply rooted joy in His life that had been missing. Most, if not all, of us have experienced the feeling of a weight being lifted from our shoulders. David felt the same way, and he rejoiced.

7

DEFENDING AGAINST OFFENSE

ONE EVENING, WHILE OUR YOUNG adult group at church was playing volleyball, I struck up a conversation with a guy I had played basketball with throughout high school. Our conversation drifted to how our high school team had played a great defense. In fact, during one game, the other team never scored against us until the beginning of the second quarter. The whole first quarter went by without a single basket for that team. (If you are not familiar with basketball, that means eight minutes of play and zero points for the other team.)

How did we shut down the other team? We played good defense. And when you play good defense, the strategies often lead to easy points for your team. If you stop the other team from scoring (that's the defense's job), your players can grab the rebound or steal the ball and get it to your end of the court. As long as the ball is on your end of the court, you have better odds of scoring points. The more points you score, the better chance you have of winning. But you cannot score points if the other team has the ball. A good defense is a must because the defense creates opportunities to go after the other team and what they stole from you (a.k.a. the ball).

Here's my theory of how basketball applies to our study on

being offended—If we build a good defense against the enemy's attacks, we open up the opportunity to deal him a defeat. To defeat the enemy, we need a great game plan. In basketball, the game plan revolves around plays and creating opportunities for ball possession and scoring. In life, that game plan or thought process focuses on never getting offended since we love the Word of God (Psalm 119:165). The enemy's goal is to derail us from all that God has for us, and carrying offense in our life is the perfect way to get derailed.

In basketball, a team practices their defensive plays every single day. They study the plays, they know how the plays work, they know where each player will be, and they know what to do when the play goes wrong. As Christians, the basic plays in our defense against being offended are:

1. Studying the Word of God and knowing how it applies to our daily life;
2. Looking forward, not backward, and
3. Living a life of no expectations.

Let's jump in and dissect those defensive plays in the next chapters so we know how to use them. The result of those plays will be a good defense because the Scripture says, "Great peace have they which love thy law, and nothing shall offend them" (Psalm 119:165). If we love the Word of God and we are consuming the Word, something in our body and our spirit changes so we become unoffendable. And being unoffendable is our game plan.

8

DEFENSIVE PLAY #1:
THE WORD

IN MATTHEW 4, JESUS WAS led by the Spirit into the wilderness to be tempted by the devil. The early verses tell us Jesus had been fasting for forty days and nights. I imagine he was hungry. I know I would be. In verse three, the tempter (Satan) comes along and says, "If you are the Son of God, command that these stones become bread." To somebody who has not eaten in forty days, the temptation to make bread would be strong. I would probably want a feast at that point, but bread would be a good deal too.

As tempting as the bread was, did Jesus give in? No. Instead, he replied, "It is written, 'Man shall not live by bread alone, but by every word that proceeds from the mouth of God.'"

After Jesus refused to turn the stone into bread, Satan tried a different tactic. "The devil took him [Jesus] up to the holy city, set him on the pinnacle of the temple, and said to him, 'If you are the Son of God, throw yourself down. For it is written: "He shall give His angels charge over you, and, in their hands they shall bear you up, lest you dash your foot against a stone"'" (verses 5 and 6).

Jesus replied using Scripture just like He did to the first

temptation—"It is written again, 'You shall not tempt the Lord your God.'"

Next, Satan takes Jesus to the top of a mountain with an amazing view. I imagine Satan sweeping His arm across the 360-degree view as he says, "All these things I give you if you fall down and worship me."

Jesus replied again with Scripture—"For it is written, 'You shall worship the Lord your God, and him only shall you serve'" (verse 10). Finally, Satan left, and the "angels came and ministered to" Jesus (verse 11).

"If you are the Son of God" are the words Satan used to try and tempt Jesus. Before Jesus's ministry actually began, Satan used the destiny of the cross and the destiny of the grave being open and Jesus walking out in freedom so we could have freedom. Satan used all the things that would come in the next three-and-a-half years because he knew if Jesus became offended at His destiny or questioned it, He would never accomplish it.

Satan came to Jesus three times, and all three times, Jesus was victorious. Jesus used Scripture to say "No, no, no. This isn't how it works. I'm called to accomplish something on earth and you aren't going to slow me down."

Many Christians, whether they are Christians for years or just a short time, encounter the tempter who plant seeds of doubt about their destiny and their ministry. Before long, they are offended that God would ask "a poor guy like me" to accomplish a mission. Immediately, in that moment, they are disqualified and their mission is aborted until they get rid of the offense.

We need to learn and employ Jesus's defense when faced with temptation. However, we cannot respond with Bible verses and love the law (the Word of God) if we do not read it. And we cannot apply verses if we do not know them. We *must* spend time in the Word, studying and learning it. If we love the Bible to the point that it becomes our defensive play against temptation, we will live out the words of Psalm 119:165—"Great peace have they which love they law, and nothing shall offend them."

We don't have to spend hours and hours every day reading chapters of the Bible. Sometimes all we need are a few verses and the time to meditate on those verses. Other ways to learn how to use the Bible as a defense include sermons, Bible study books, and even praise and worship music. One word of warning—do not use all the other ways and neglect actually sitting down and reading or listening to the Bible.

9

DEFENSIVE PLAY #2: LOOKING FORWARD

HERE'S A SCENARIO FOR YOU—YOU'RE driving down the road and your toddler starts screaming in the back seat. What do you do? You quickly glance over your shoulder and then stretch your neck to look in the rearview mirror. As you focus intently on the rearview mirror, the car drifts a little to the left. Your speed slows down. You glance out the windshield again, and at the last second, spot that indecisive squirrel in your lane. You swerve, and your toddler's screams escalate. You look in the rearview mirror again, and without thinking about it, you watch the mirror more than the road in front of you.

In life, some people's rearview mirrors are bigger than their windshields. They dwell in the past. "That person said or did _____ to me and I'm still upset at them" or "I should've _____." They start conversations with "I remember when _____" and then launch into a long trip down memory lane. Nothing is wrong with memories and sharing them with others. The problem is when the focus is continually on the past rather than the present. If someone offended us twenty years ago, no matter the type of offense, those memories bring up the offense and all its baggage. As a result, we fail to live in the present with eyes on the prize. If we are not paying attention to what is ahead of us and instead focus on an offense that already happened, the hours and days of life move forward without us.

Do you remember the story of Lot's wife in the Old Testament? She is the one who looked back on the way out of Sodom and Gomorrah and God turned her into a pillar of salt. In the New Testament, a single verse in Luke 17 is dedicated to the phrase "Remember Lot's wife." Why would Jesus say those words?

Luke 17 starts by telling us "It is impossible that no offenses should come." And then thirty-one verses later, we are told to remember Lot's wife. Putting together those facts, do you think maybe Lot's wife was offended or living in offense? The Old Testament does not tell us the details about why she looked back. Maybe she was mad at Lot for making her leave her friends. Maybe she was offended at God for destroying what she thought was the perfect place to live. When we get to heaven, we'll find out more details about why she looked back, but for now, it is enough to know that her focus was not on the right spot—where she was going—and God turned her into a pillar of salt.

We have already established that we are going to be tempted by offense at some point. It is going to happen. We cannot avoid it. Jesus used the word *impossible*, so we know somewhere somehow we will encounter offense. Once we give in and pick up an offense, that offense steals our attention from what is in front of us and focuses it on what is behind us or what already happened. We look in the rearview mirror at what the person said or did. We rehearse the events in our mind. And we fail to pay attention to what is in front of us. Because we are not focusing on our windshield, we run smack into unforgiveness, bitterness, and a host of other negative emotions and complications. Lot's wife looked back at what was behind her and she lost her inheritance and her destiny.

Keep looking forward, not behind or in the rearview mirror.

10

DEFENSIVE PLAY #3:
NO EXPECTATIONS

JESUS WALKED THE SAME PLANET as us. He dealt with the same human emotions and conflicts as us. He had plenty of chances to be offended every single day, yet He lived His whole life on earth without ever being offended. He was unoffendable. Pretty impressive, right? But how did Jesus remain unoffendable?

We already know two defenses He employed—quoting Scripture to defend against temptation and never staring in His rearview mirror. Beyond those two things, how was Jesus different from us and able to walk through all kinds of offenses and not pick any up? It's simple—He had no expectations of mankind.

If Jesus had expectations of man, He would have been disappointed. The disciples, a group of twelve men who traveled with Jesus, gave Him every opportunity to be offended, yet He never was. He knew if He had expectations of His disciples, He would set himself up for offense. Think about Peter and Judas—

Jesus said, "Peter, you'll deny me."

"Oh no, no, no. I'll die for you. I'll go to prison for you."

Twenty-three verses later, the Bible tells us Peter said, "Woman, I don't know Him."

At the same time that Peter was promising he would not deny

Jesus, Judas, another of the disciples, was preparing to betray Jesus to the chief priests and guard. Judas, a man whom Jesus trusted as His financial guy for years, tossed their friendship to the side for thirty pieces of silver. Hours before the betrayal, Judas sat at the same table as Peter and agreed that he would never deny Jesus.

Judas's betrayal was the catalyst that led to Jesus's death on the cross less than twenty-four hours later. Knowing that fact, I think we can all agree that Jesus had every human right to be offended at Judas and his actions. If Jesus had any expectation of Judas repenting for his betrayal, Jesus would have opened up the opportunity for offense. But without that expectation, Jesus was able to continue His mission on earth. That lack of expectation combined with His servant's heart allowed Him to fulfill the mission God called Him to.

Before Peter's denial and Judas's betrayal, Jesus went to Nazareth and told the people, "Listen, I'm here to bring the best that I have for you. You're my people." The end of Matthew 13 tells us, "He taught them in their synagogue, so that they were astonished and said, 'Where did this man get this wisdom and these mighty works?'" I imagine it was like when we meet someone who impresses us and we think, "Wow! They're so smart. Their words are amazing!"—that's what was happening in Nazareth.

Then some guy sitting in the back stands up and hollers, "Hey, isn't that the carpenter's son?" At that moment, the anointing left the crowd because the people stopped seeing Jesus as the one bringing truth and wisdom from heaven and instead started seeing him as the carpenter's little kid.

"Is not His mother called Mary and His brothers James, Joses, Simon, and Judas? And His sisters, are they not all with us? Where then did this man get all these things? So they were offended at him" (verses 55–57). The people were blind to Jesus's assignment and didn't understand what He was on earth to do. Instead, all they saw Him as was the carpenter's son and that fact offended them. When someone is offended at us and they make it known, how hard is it to not pick up an offense against that person? That's the situation Jesus was in. He had the opportunity to pick up the offense, but He refused it.

If Jesus expected the people of Nazareth to accept Him as more than the carpenter's son, He would have been offended, but He did not have that expectation. If Jesus expected Satan to give in or apologize for trying to tempt Him in the wilderness, He would have been offended. But He was not. The religious people ridiculed Jesus every day, and He should have been offended. But He was not.

Jump forward to today. We would fail miserably if God had expectations of us. Here's the good news—He has no expectations. We studied Genesis 1:27 in an earlier chapter and looked at how God has already blessed us. Those blessings come with no strings attached. We do not have to meet certain criteria or goals before God blesses us. No, He blesses us first and then gives the command to "be fruitful and multiply." And if God blesses us, we have the anointing to do what He asks of us. If Jesus lived a life of no expectations and never had an offense with anyone, we can learn from His example.

Think about all the offenses in your life, even the ones you have already dealt with and sought forgiveness for. What caused the offense? (I'll give you a hint: The correct answer isn't someone's name or what they did or said.)

The root or cause of every single offense is misdiagnosed or unfilled expectations. Let me repeat that. The offenses you have carried throughout your life come from unrealized expectations. Have you ever heard or said these statements: "They should have known better" or "I expected more out of them"? I imagine all of us have said those things at some point. When those statements leave our lips, we set ourselves up to be offended because our expectations are not met.

If we carry expectations for people, we will be offended

because someone somewhere will fail to meet our expectations. When our spouse does not do what we think he or she is supposed to do, that expectation sets us up for offense. (I guarantee that if you talk to any divorce attorney, they will say that marriages fail because of unfulfilled expectations.) When we naturally expect a relationship to be free of abusive behavior, and the other person betrays that expectation, offense takes root. When a church splits, the root of the split is unmet expectations. People expected the pastor or the leadership to lead a certain way. Or they expected the sermons to be on a certain topic or the music to sound a certain way. No matter the cause of the split, it all goes back to unmet expectations.

Don't let expectations take over your life. You see, some of us have been offended in life and, as a result, stopped being fruitful in the kingdom. God's plan was for us to never stop but rather push on and on to do what He called us to do—even if the climate isn't right and even if it means that we are hanging on a pole like martyrs of the past. It does not matter. His plan for us is to push on.

Christians throughout history have done everything God told them to do, never stopping and never getting offended. How? Because they did not have expectations about people; instead they had expectations about a Savior. Do not expect things from human beings. Just expect things from God, our heavenly father, because He is really good. And when He says to go do something, we must go do it and allow Him to take care of us all along the way. Will it cost something to keep going and not stop? Probably, but we can rest in the promise that we'll be safe and taken care of.

Offense from unmet expectations is the one thing that holds the church back. It is the one thing that splits churches. It is the one thing that keeps people from their destiny. It is the one thing that locks our anointing inside of us. If we are going to have expectations, know that expectations about people are the breeding ground for offense. If we have expectations about God, it is a breeding ground for miracles.

Do you want to be bound up or do you want to experience miracles? It is your choice. If you choose miracles, surrender those things that are holding you back. Maybe it is an offense that happened from your perspective, but it did not actually happen to you. Maybe you have unmet expectations. Lay it all down at Jesus's feet and be free. Be unstoppable and unoffendable.

CASE STUDY #3

PAUL AND JOHN THE BAPTIST

W E HAVE LOOKED BRIEFLY AT Paul's teaching already, but let's study how he handled offense in His own life. In Acts 24, Paul is standing before Felix, the governor, and defending himself against some serious accusations. A man by the name of Tertullus accused Paul of causing problems in the temple, practicing a different religion, and more.

> Then Paul, after the governor had nodded to him to speak, answered: "Inasmuch as I know that you have been for many years a judge of this nation, I do the more cheerfully answer for myself, because you may ascertain that it is no more than twelve days since I went up to Jerusalem to worship. And they neither found me in the temple disputing with anyone nor inciting the crowd, either in the synagogues or in the city. Nor can they prove the things of which they now accuse me. But this I confess to you, that according to the Way which they call a sect, so I worship the God of my fathers, believing all things which are written in the Law and in the Prophets. I have hope in God, which they themselves also accept, that there will be a resurrection of the dead, both of the just and the unjust. This being so, I myself always

strive to have a conscience without offense toward God and men." (vv. 10–16)

Did you catch that last part? Paul, a man who accomplished great things and was healed, delivered, and set free by Jesus, is defending himself and says, "Listen, all the things I just defended myself about, that is all good and well. But I have to work on myself every single day so I'm not offended at God and at you. I know that, if I'm offended at God and if I'm offended at you, all the other things that I just described about myself and defended myself for, they all mean nothing. It means absolutely nothing if I'm offended at God or offended at men."

Stop and think about that. Paul, a man who wrote a significant portion of the New Testament and who God pulled out of darkness and into marvelous light, says, in our words of today, "I have to guard my heart every single day so I'm not offended at God for where I am or offended at you for what you are doing."

Did you catch the words "every single day"? In the Scripture, he uses the words "always strive" or all the time. The temptation for offense will always be there, even when we are in the toughest spots. No matter what we have accomplished, we have to be like Paul and do our due diligence and the hard work to remain unoffendable. We must remain free of offense with those who accuse us, those who lie about us, and those who make choices contrary to what we believe and what the Bible says. We have to guard our heart.

John the Baptist is another Bible hero who encountered offense and spoke about it when he was in a tough spot. He was a righteous and godly man who dressed a little odd and ate weird stuff, but according to Matthew 11, nobody was greater than him.

Now it came to pass, when Jesus finished commanding His twelve disciples, that He departed from there to teach and to preach in their cities. And when John had heard in prison about the works of Christ, he sent two of His disciples and said to Him, "Are You the Coming One, or do we look for another?" (Matthew 11:1–3)

Before we read further in the chapter, let's put those verses into context. John the Baptist is sitting in prison and knows His life might be ending soon. With nothing to do and plenty of time on His hands, he starts questioning everything he did in the past. "Did I really do the right thing? Is that guy I gave my whole life for the real deal?" John the Baptist, the man who called out Jesus and led the way for Him, is struggling. Unable to talk directly to Jesus Himself, John sends a couple of messengers to Jesus with those questions.

"Jesus answered and said to them, 'Go and tell John the things which you hear and see:'"

And then, instead of giving a statement of love and appreciation to John the Baptist, He says, "Tell him that everything that he has seen is proof that I am who I am. 'The blind see and the lame walk; the lepers are cleansed and the deaf hear; the dead are raised up and the poor have the gospel preached to them.'" Jesus doesn't stop there even though that statement would've been enough proof for John. He adds, "And blessed is he who is not offended because of me."

Jesus knows John the Baptist had plenty of opportunity to be offended at God, but he never picked up the offense. John was the forerunner, the one who led the way, but he never said, "Look at me, people! I did these things to prepare for this man you love so much. Follow me instead." No, he continually pointed others to Jesus and did not allow offense at God or man to get in the way. And now he is sitting in prison staring at death because he called out sin.

Matthew 14:1–5 recaps the story that led to John the Baptist's imprisonment and eventual beheading:

At that time Herod the tetrarch heard the report about

Jesus and said to His servants, "This is John the Baptist; he is risen from the dead, and therefore these powers are at work in him." For Herod had laid hold of John and bound him, and put him in prison for the sake of Herodias, His brother Philip's wife. Because John had said to him, "It is not lawful for you to have her." And although he wanted to put him to death, he feared the multitude, because they counted him as a prophet.

John the Baptist had the audacity to say to Herod, the ruler at the time, that the marriage he was in was wrong. John spoke the truth and ended up with His head on a platter because of it, but he did it because speaking the truth is the right thing to do all the time. He defined marriage according to what Scripture said, not what civil authority said.

If we are supposed to be the pure bride of Christ awaiting the King of Kings, we can see in John a picture of what we are to do. John was not the one sitting in the back saying, "I'll let someone else speak that. It's okay that the pastor says that, but I don't want to do that." No, John stood up and took a righteous stand on truth, knowing the consequences, because the Word of the Lord, righteousness, and true holiness were more important than caving to the whims of people who needed delivered and set free. And we already know that taking a stand led to John being martyred.

A time is coming when you may need to be prosecuted for your beliefs in the kingdom of God. The days will be as dark as night. Now is the time to examine yourself like Paul and John the Baptist. Can you say you are free of offense? Can you say you are working hard every single day to not be offended at man and God?

11

FINDING OFFENSES

I HAVE A CHALLENGE FOR you that will lead to transformation in your life. But before I tell you the challenge, let's review what you have learned so far. You understand or are trying to understand what offense is and how serious offense is in your life. You know you can be offended not only at man but also God, and you learned about strategies for defending against offense.

What we have not talked about is how to find offenses that already exist. This chapter and the challenge detail that process, and then the next chapter dives into offering forgiveness for offenses. You may want to continue reading through the next chapter, or even the rest of the book, before completing the challenge; however, you *must* take the challenge if you want your life to be transformed. So, what is the challenge?

My challenge is for you to ask God three questions (and I will share those questions shortly). For some of you, these questions may take a couple of hours to work through. For others, it may take a full day or three days or a week because you have decades of offenses to deal with. Every person is different, and it is important to take as much time as you need.

To start the challenge, you need to do something that might be difficult. Take your phone, hold down the button on the side, and turn it off. Then carry it outside and put it somewhere safe—in your car, on a shelf in the shed, under a cushion on the porch. The goal is for it to be out of the house and not a distraction. Once you have stashed your phone somewhere safe, walk back inside your house and pick up your Bible and a notebook. Go to a quiet place and sit down with Jesus. Grab a glass of water on your way if you have to because you will be spending a couple of hours in your quiet place. Once you have settled in, talk to Jesus and ask Him these questions:

1. Am I offended at you, God?

   Write down what God tells you, and then deal with it. Do not skip that last part—Deal with what God tells you. You can say, "Lord, I'm offended with you about _____. Show me how to release that offense. Show me how to never carry that offense with you ever again. I don't want to go back to this place I'm at right now." And as you rest in the stillness of your quiet place, God will tell you exactly what you need to do.

2. Am I offended at a person?

   When you ask this question, be prepared for what is coming. God's going to give you a list of names and offenses because He tells us not to be offended at Him or man. Write down the names. For some people this list will be one page; for others, it will be three pages or longer. My list was two-and-a-half pages, and I discovered offenses I did not know I carried. Offenses sometimes are under the ground—we don't know we are offended at someone until God shows us. Then we have to dig up that offense and deal with it through prayer:

   "Father, I forgive [name] for what they did to me. They [hurt me, rejected me, etc.]. I ask that You forgive me too and that there are no charges against them and no record of it in heaven. I forgive them as freely as you forgive me. Please forgive me for hating them, rejecting them, and for hardening my heart toward You. Devil, you have used this to gain access to my life and to bring me into bondage. I have given you authority in that part of my life, but now I tell you, you have no more authority over me. I have given my life to Jesus. In Jesus's name, Amen."

When you pray that prayer, burdens will roll off you. You will tangibly feel those weights lifted. Your shoulders are going to go back further, no longer stooped under the weight of offense. And you will hold your head higher.

Don't be surprised if you go to church the next Sunday and see someone and think, "Oh, I never knew I was offended at them. Now I can actually look them in the eyes, and I don't have to avoid them in the lobby." It happens, and it is a beautiful thing.

One word of caution: When you see people from your list on the street, at church, or wherever, be wise. You cannot think "Oh, that person did _____ to me twenty years ago and I've forgiven them. Everything's good now. I don't feel that angst anymore, so I want to go hang out with them." No, use wisdom and healthy boundaries. Matthew 10 tells us to be "wise as serpents and harmless as doves" for a reason. Be friendly, but do not expect anything in return.

3. God, how do I build an unoffendable life?

"Lord, teach me in this moment how to build a life that is unoffendable from this point forward. Show me personally how to set up my life structure so I am unoffendable when offenses come. How do I deal with offenses in a healthy way? Show me. Show me who I am when I'm not offended."

God will reveal to you what you are like when you are not snippy at other people, when you are not holding grudges against others, and when you are not speaking negatively about others because you are offended at them. That person is who God sees you as and who He called you to be, not the person who is grumpy or better than others or bitter and unfruitful.

When you receive that revelation of who you are without offense, take steps to build an unoffendable life. Use the defensive strategies we talked about. I cannot promise that building this kind of life will be easy. Satan will tempt you, and the more productive you are in the kingdom, the more he will attack. Use God's Word and keep looking forward every single day.

After you work through those questions, take it all to the cross, never to pick it up ever again. Once you have placed that list of names at the cross, worship like you have never worshipped before. All the weight you have carried for decades— gone. All the control and trying to manipulate other people to get what you want—gone. Walk in that freedom you have never felt before. Shout praises from the rooftops. Fall on your knees in adoration. Sing, dance, and worship.

12

FORGIVING OFFENSE

HAVE YOU TRIED TO LIVE an unoffendable life, but you gave in to the temptation and picked up an offense? Take a deep breath and don't feel bad. It's not the end of the world. Every single person who reads this book fits into one of two categories—Either they will be tempted by offense in the future or they're already walking around carrying an offense with all its baggage. So, now that we know what offense is and its dangers, what do we do when we pick up an offense? How do we process and reverse the offense?

In the previous chapter, I gave you a challenge that's great for discovering underground offenses we do not know we are carrying around. But sometimes we get caught up in life and walk straight into an offense. Five minutes later, we know we are offended, we realize it, and we own it, but what should we do next?

First, we dig through all the religious stuff we have been taught and go back to what Jesus taught us, you know, the red letters in the Gospels. We have to learn how to process an offense as Jesus did and through His words. The red letters are awesome, even if they mean correction to our soul.

Second, we offer forgiveness. We have already studied parts

of Luke 17 in previous chapters, but let's look at the first four verses again:

> Then He said to the disciples, "It is impossible that no offenses should come, but woe to him through whom they do come! It would be better for him if a millstone were hung around His neck, and he were thrown into the sea, than that he should offend one of these little ones. Take heed to yourselves. If your brother sins against you, rebuke him; and if he repents, forgive him. And if he sins against you seven times in a day, and seven times in a day returns to you, saying, 'I repent,' you shall forgive him."

In verse five, the disciples' response is interesting. When Jesus said to forgive people, the disciples responded with "Increase our faith!" Did they ask for their faith to be increased when Jesus told them to go heal the sick, raise the dead, and cast out demons? No, they went out and did what He commanded. Now in verse five, they ask for an increase in faith after Jesus tells them to forgive others. They're basically saying, "We can handle going out and casting out demons and all that, but we can't handle forgiving seven times." The disciples' response should be enough for us to realize that forgiving an offense isn't easy.

Matthew 18, a parallel chapter to Luke 17, tells us Peter couldn't help but question what Jesus had said. Peter went back after the events of Luke 17 and says, "Hey, do you really mean seven times?"

If you read into what Peter is saying, I think His words are more like "Okay, I will forgive John seven times, but on the eighth time, I'm sticking a dagger in His side" or maybe "Okay, seven times. I get it, Jesus. But on the eighth time, he's going to get it." Another way of looking at Peter's question is "Can I be justified living in malice toward someone? Well, you know, if I follow through with your plan?"

How often are we like Peter and present our interpretation of what the Lord says to see if it is right? Sometimes the Lord shows or tells us something and we can't help but ask, "For real? You really want me to _____?"

Jesus, who could've been offended at Peter's response but was not, replies with "I do not say to you up to seven times, but up to seventy times seven" (Matthew 18:22). Wow. Of all the people I have met in my lifetime, I don't know anyone who can offend me over 490 times in one day. But, if it were possible, is Jesus saying that on the 491st time, I could stick it to the person who offended me? Or if the person can do it in twenty-four hours, I can stick it to that person, right? No, that's not what Jesus is saying at all.

Jesus is saying in all things, forgive. Think about that famous verse Jesus says from the cross—"Father, forgive them for they know not what they do."

Forgiveness is the key to fruitfulness. When we are offended and start to experience unfruitfulness in our life, we need to forgive. It doesn't matter how many times someone offends us or even if they don't know what they've done to us, we need to forgive. Jesus says, "Listen, it doesn't matter if you pick up 490 of these offenses, forgive."

Did you notice that Jesus didn't say "forgive *and* forget"? He never said to "forget" when He told Peter to forgive "up to seventy times seven" because He knew the idea of forgetting would lead many people into failing to forgive others. Living a life of forgiveness does not mean that we forget. There are simply some things we cannot and should not forget.

If we forget what has been done to us, we experience spiritual amnesia and set ourselves up for failure and additional trauma. Maybe a woman cannot forget what her brother did to her when she was five. Or someone cannot forget what their ex-wife or ex-husband did to them. Because the church has misinterpreted Jesus's command to forgive and added the word *forget*, these people never take that step toward forgiveness because they cannot forget the ugliness they endured. As a result, they never experience healing and they carry that burden with them for the rest of their lives.

If Jesus isn't saying "forgive *and* forget," what is He saying? Forgive, and in your forgiveness, find healing in the situation you are in. When that memory comes back, do not attack that person again, and do not hold malice against them. Forgive. We can forgive anybody, no matter how heinous the thing they did against us was. Forgive and be free.

If you are reading this today and have struggled to forgive because you cannot get that certain thing out of your mind, you are in the wrong. You need to be healed. The way to healing is through releasing that burden and seeking forgiveness. Is there biblical proof for the idea of forgiveness leading to healing? Paul's words in Philippians 3:12–14 say,

> Not that I have already attained, or am already perfected; but I press on, that I may lay hold of that for which Christ Jesus has also laid hold of me. Brethren, I do not count myself to have apprehended; but one thing I do, forgetting those things which are behind and reaching forward to those things which are ahead, I press toward the goal for the prize of the upward call of God in Christ Jesus.

I know a few of you are saying, "Woah. Wait a second, Pastor Rob. You just contradicted yourself. You said we can't forget the things in our past or we'll be in trouble, but Paul just said he forgets those things." Okay, I see where you are coming from because it does sound like a contradiction. When Paul says he forgets those things, he does not mean he wiped out the memories. In the Book of Acts, Paul gives His testimony in court, and based on that testimony, we know that he clearly remembers the things of His past and what he did to the church. When Paul uses the word *forget*, I believe he means he left those events in the past and he is no longer bound by those things. He sought forgiveness and received healing. He was able to use those events in His testimony so others could come to know Jesus, experience healing, and move on. He always remembered what happened in the past, but he used His past to further God's kingdom.

Besides "forgetting," there's one other thing that comes with forgiveness that sometimes trips us up—trust. We have been taught or we think that if we forgive someone, we have to trust them. No, just like "forgive and forget" isn't biblical, neither is "forgive and trust." We don't have to forgive someone and immediately trust them (or ever trust them) because some people just cannot be trusted. Boundaries are acceptable.

Did you know that God doesn't trust us? He does not trust you, and He does not trust me. The parable of the talents is in Matthew 25, and this story illustrates this idea of trust. In verse twenty-one, the master says to the servant, "Well done. You were faithful over a few things; I will put you in charge of many things." The servant earned the master's trust by demonstrating how well he could care for the five talents the master gave him. In other words, trust is one of those things that is earned. Right after we accept Jesus as Savior, God doesn't say, "I trust you with the mountaintop, so here take it." No, He does not do that. He tells us we have to grow in our faith and in the wisdom of God just like children grow. And as we grow, His trust in us grows. If God doesn't trust us, why do we as believers think we have to go back and trust others with an unwavering trust after we have forgiven them for unimaginable offenses? If they have broken our trust, they do not immediately receive our trust again.

Jesus, in both Luke 17 and Matthew 18, does not give us any qualifiers for forgiveness. Neither passage says we need to forget or need to trust before we can forgive. All we need to do is forgive, forgive, forgive. If you have people in your life that you have not forgiven because you cannot forget and you cannot trust them, do not be bound by religious untruth. Seek forgiveness as God intended it. Simply forgive—no forgetting or trusting is necessary.

One thing we all know is that sometimes forgiveness is hard. It hurts. It takes humility. And if we forgive someone in our flesh, it will come back to haunt us. So, if forgiveness isn't about forgetting and trusting and we can't forgive in the flesh, what is this idea of forgiveness really about? Is it about us? No, it is not.

Forgiveness is about faith. It takes a level of faith that maybe we do not have. However, we can tap into the One who *is* faith. We can take Jesus's faith and say two things, one to the person we are forgiving and one to God:

- "I, in faith, forgive you. I'm going to be free of this offense. You can do whatever you want with my forgiveness, but I'm going to be free to walk through my life and minister to others."

- "Listen, Jesus, I have received love and forgiveness from you. I'm taking that love and forgiveness and I'm extending it toward [the other person's name]."

The extent to which we can forgive others shows what we have received from God. If we do not understand the forgiveness and love we receive from God, we cannot extend that same forgiveness to people around us. Those who have received the fullness of the love of God are called the remnant in the Bible. They have received forgiveness for sin and forgiveness for everything they have ever done past, present, and future. And then they turn around and give that forgiveness to other people.

When we have truly forgiven someone, our heart is free and we can serve others, including those we have extended forgiveness to. Remember, we don't have to forget what they have done or trust them in order to give them food when they need food or pray for them when life has them down. We can minister in love and faith like God called us to do and not trust them.

CASE STUDY #5

PARABLE OF THE UNFORGIVING SERVANT

I N THE PREVIOUS CHAPTER, I mentioned that Matthew 18 is the parallel chapter to Luke 17. And we know from earlier in this book that Luke 17 is the chapter where Jesus teaches about offense. So with that context, let's look at the story of the unforgiving servant in Matthew 18:21–34.

> Then Peter came to Him and said, "Lord, how often shall my brother sin against me, and I forgive him? Up to seven times?"
>
> Jesus said to him, 'I do not say to you, up to seven times, but up to seventy times seven. Therefore the kingdom of heaven is like a certain king who wanted to settle accounts with His servants. And when he had begun to settle accounts, one was brought to him who owed him ten thousand talents. But as he was not able to pay, His master commanded that he be sold, with His wife and children and all that he had, and that payment be made.
>
> The servant therefore fell down before him, saying, "Master, have patience with me, and I will pay you all."
>
> Then the master of that servant was moved with compassion, released him, and forgave him the debt.

The servant's sentence—the command to be sold—was already spoken as payment for the debt, but then the master changed the servant's sentence. Does that sound familiar to you? It is the story of the gospel. Think back to the early chapters of Genesis. Once Adam and Eve sinned, mankind was sentenced to death. And then the Master changed the sentence. Jesus came, took away that debt on the cross, and offered man eternal life. The Master changed the sentence! Hallelujah!

> But that servant went out and found one of His fellow servants who owed him a hundred denarii; and he laid hands on him and took him by the throat, saying, "Pay me what you owe!"
>
> So His fellow servant fell down at His feet and begged him, saying, "Have patience with me, and I will pay you all."
>
> And he would not, but went and threw him into prison till he should pay the debt.
>
> So when His fellow servants saw what had been done, they were very grieved, and came and told their master all that had been done.
>
> Then His master, after he had called him, said to him, "You wicked servant! I forgave you all that debt because you begged me. Should you not also have had compassion on your fellow servant, just as I had pity on you?" And His master was angry, and delivered him to the torturers until he should pay all that was due to him.
>
> So my heavenly father also will do to you if each of you, from His heart, does not forgive His brother His trespasses.

Through the parable, Jesus is saying "Listen, there's forgiveness from heaven for your sins—past, present, and future. They're already paid for. Every mistake. Everything. Every broken piece is already covered. But you cannot live a fruitful life if you do not receive all of that. You can only be as fruitful as much as you receive from the Father."

Sadly, many people walk around with a low limit of forgiveness because they have not received a big portion from the Father. And the Father does not lack in wanting to give us forgiveness. We have been forgiven by the creator of the universe for every angry word we said today, for the attitude we had, for the cuss word we uttered under our breath, for the lie we told. For all of it, God forgives us. In fact, He forgave us before we even sinned. He died on the cross to take all those sins long before we were ever born.

If we could just grab hold of and understand the greatness of God's love and forgiveness toward us, we would be different humans on this earth. We would spread God's love, a contagious love with forgiveness, far and wide. In Philippians 1, Paul tells us all these things are going on in His life, but His one goal is that Christ is magnified.

If we walk around in unforgiveness, people are only seeing you and me. If we walk around in forgiveness over and over, people see Christ. And showing Christ to others should be every Christian's goal.

One other important point in this parable is in the final verse—"So my heavenly father also will do to you if each of you, from His heart, does not forgive His brother His trespasses." What does that mean? The previous verse talks about how the master sent the servant to be tortured by the jailers all because the servant failed to forgive. Then Jesus draws the parallel to our life. The servant was tortured physically, but our torture isn't something that comes from the outside. It is something that actually bubbles up from the inside. When we are unforgiving of someone for the debt they owe, something rises up on the inside and begins to torment us. Our mind goes around and around and around. The problem is not someone else. It is not the offense. It is not the person that committed the offense against us. The problem is us until we offer forgiveness.

Maybe you are someone who says "I just cannot forgive. It

is not because of the offense and what that person did or what I did. I just can't do it." Again, it is your problem, not God's. The more you open up to the Lord, the more you receive of Him. The more time you spend with Him, the more you understand how much He loves you and the more you cannot contain all He has given you.

The inability to forgive is rooted in what you have not received. The enemy wants you distracted. He wants you looking in the rearview mirror. He wants you to put a cap on what God will give you and say, "You know, forgiveness only goes up to this point." Satan's lies are not true. God's love and forgiveness are so expansive they cannot be contained. And the more you receive of His love and forgiveness, the more you can offer to others.

13

PROCESSING OFFENSE
AND FORGIVENESS

Nот LONG AFTER I ASKED God to show me the people I was offended with, I had the following conversation with God. I cannot divulge the circumstances that led to this conversation, but the conversation itself should be enough.

God: Rob, you are offended at {insert name}.

Me: What? There's no way I'm offended. I cannot be offended at {insert name}. I love them. Our relationship is awesome. I'm not offended.

God: No. You *are* offended.

Me: At what?

God: At something you heard about them.

Me: I didn't even give that a second thought in my mind. The whole thing was crazy.

God: Yep, but it stuck, and now you are offended.

Within five minutes of that conversation, I sent a text to the person asking to talk with them because I had some stuff I was processing that the Lord revealed to me. I met with the person, and we had the most amazing conversation. When I got back in my truck after the meeting, I said to the Lord, "What would that meeting have looked like, Lord, if I didn't get rid of that offense?"

Sometimes all the enemy needs is one little innocent comment that you don't even know is stewing inside of you, and before you know it, you are carrying around offense. If it happens to me, I'm positive it happens to you. So how do we position ourselves if we pick up an offense that we should not have?

Processing offense means having an open heart and allowing the Lord to speak truth to you and adjust your attitude. If you have that open heart, He will change you. If you don't, you will remain the same and walk around with offense that you don't even know is there. That offense gives the enemy a pathway inside to challenge your destiny and distract you from what you are called to do. And I'm sure you do not want that.

In Chapter Three, we studied the three types of offense—imaginary, accidental, and purposeful. The first two, imaginary and accidental, are offenses we create. We "think" someone meant their words a certain way, but we don't say anything to the person or confront them. We simply decide to be offended at what they said.

Imaginary and accidental offenses are the easiest for us to process. We created the offense, so we need to find the root of the problem within ourselves and work through those unmet expectations.

Purposeful offenses, the third type of offense, are different. These offenses are the ones someone committed against us intentionally. They meant to harm us. Processing a purposeful offense is harder because another person who knowingly offended us is involved. We could tell that person they owe us and they need to repay all they stole from us, except we learned that purposeful offenders often do not apologize or make the situation right.

Some of us are bound up in life because we have expected an apology from someone who hurt us and we are never going to get that apology. Maybe that person is still alive, maybe they're not, but they're not going to give us an apology no matter what. Imagine this scenario:

> One day, I receive a call to speak at your funeral. During the service, I talk about how you lived life and all the things you enjoyed. And then a family member steps up to the microphone and says, "Man, there was this one thing that held him back in life. His Uncle Joe never apologized for what he did to him years ago. And because of this thing that happened, he lived an unfruitful life. He was waiting for an apology, but Uncle Joe never apologized."

Could someone say those words at your funeral? Are you unfruitful or stuck in life because you are waiting for an apology? If Jesus were to wait for an apology from all the people who could have offended him, He would still be waiting. We have to show our maturity and understand that man is broken. We have to deal with the brokenness. (In the above scenario, the brokenness is someone else's inability to apologize, but the brokenness may show up in other ways.) Once we deal with the brokenness, we can move on. The other person may be stuck, but we are not. We are free to live out the mission God called us to.

So how do we deal with the brokenness and lack of apology? Matthew 18 tells us to forgive. And if you look closely, that's all it says. It does not say trust or forget, just simply forgive. However, sometimes we forgive a person for an offense, and the guilt and torment come back. The problem is we forgave in the flesh, not in faith. In our offer of forgiveness, we said to our offender "You owe me." However, true forgiveness is done in faith saying "You do not owe me anything. Your debt is forgiven."

The servant in Matthew 18 had the full forgiveness of His

master, but he did not know how to take that forgiveness and transfer it to the people who were serving him. We can say we have the forgiveness of the Father, but if we don't know how to process offense and use forgiveness, we will be stuck in that place of torment. We can have all the forgiveness of sin and be totally fresh and clean, yet fail to transfer and demonstrate forgiveness to the next generation if we don't know how to process an offense and offer forgiveness.

I'm sure a few of you are scratching your heads and wondering exactly how to offer true forgiveness. Sure, "offer true forgiveness and process the offense" looks simple enough in writing, but how do you *actually* forgive the offense, that debt the offender owes you?

Step one is to receive the forgiveness of the Father. Don't start off by running to your offender, pouring salt on the table, and all that. No, you have to receive from the Father *all* the love and forgiveness He offers you. When you receive forgiveness, as the servant did, you stand in a whole new light. If all the people reading this book had their mortgage paid off (forgiven) and every bill paid for the rest of their lives, they would look at life differently, right? This world would have more smiles in it. Our churches would have more people and more smiles. Why do we not react the same way because Jesus paid it all and forgave every single debt we owe Him?

Step two is to remember you are free of debt. Jesus does not hold anything against you. God the Father does not hold anything against you. You are free and clear in the kingdom of God, nothing owed to anyone. Jesus gave His life for our debt, and we cannot forget that.

Step three is to release other people from their debt. You can't walk up to them and say, "You owe me." No, now you walk up to them and say, "I love you. I may not trust you, but I love you." I know that's hard to swallow because we have been taught that we have to trust people after we forgive them, but we don't.

We can say "I love you, but I will not let you near my kids" and everything will be okay.

Step four is to vow to yourself that you will never go back to the torment that was on you before you offered forgiveness. The enemy wants to dump that torment back on you. He wants to say nothing happened and you never forgave that person. Do not believe His lies. Purpose in your heart that the torment that comes will no longer stay and that you are going to walk in freedom.

If you've stuck with me throughout this book, you might be thinking "If processing forgiveness is truly that easy, why don't people forgive offenses and release people from their debt more often?" It's because we believe a false idea. We think that if we release the other person, they got away with what they did. If I forgive that family member who did that thing to me back in 1994, he got away with it. If I forgive my ex-wife or my ex-husband for what they did to me, they got away with it. Well, I have some news for you—you are the only one who is stuck.

Forgiving the other person does not mean that person gets away with what happened. They have to answer to the good judge one day. "Vengeance is mine, says the Lord." Do not keep yourself bound up in offense and fail to forgive others because you believe a false idea about forgiveness. God will deal with the offender.

Productivity (fruit-bearing) only happens when we process the offense and offer forgiveness. As long as we hang on to the offense, our life will be barren like David's Michal because holding on to debt makes us unproductive and unfruitful. Release the offense today. Lean into the truth that Jesus paid it all. His blood covers everything. All the offenses. All the guilt. All the shame. All the torment. He paid it all. Dwell in God's love and offer His forgiveness to those who have wronged you.

14

BE MADE WHOLE

Now Peter and John went up together to the temple at the hour of prayer, the ninth hour. And a certain man lame from His mother's womb was carried, whom they laid daily at the gate of the temple which is called Beautiful, to ask alms from those who entered the temple; who, seeing Peter and John about to go into the temple, asked for alms.

And fixing His eyes on him, with John, Peter said, "Look at us."

So he gave them His attention, expecting to receive something from them.

Then Peter said, "Silver and gold I do not have, but what I do have I give you: In the name of Jesus Christ of Nazareth, rise up and walk." And he took him by the right hand and lifted him up, and immediately His feet and ankle bones received strength.

So he, leaping up, stood and walked and entered the temple with them—walking, leaping, and praising God. And all the people saw him walking and praising God. Then they knew that it was he who sat begging alms at the Beautiful Gate of the temple; and they were filled with wonder and amazement at what had happened to him. (Acts 3:1–10)

The lame man is sort of like the man by the pool, right? This man had the opportunity to be offended because he'd had an ailment since His birth, and every day, someone took him to the gate. Jesus, the man who was healing those who were sick, had walked through that same gate about two-and-a-half years earlier. The lame man likely heard about Jesus's miracles and watched Jesus walk right by him on His way into the temple.

Wow, stop and think about that—Jesus walked by, healing people on His way, but never healed the lame man. Have you figured out where this is going? Do you think the lame man had an opportunity to be offended? He'd had a legitimate ailment since birth, yet the Miracle Healer walked right by him. In my mind, that's plenty of opportunity for offense, but the lame man was not offended. Like the man by the pool, he went back every day, just waiting patiently for His turn.

Then along comes Peter and John. Peter tells the man to look at them, and the man looks up "expecting to receive something from them." When you are offended at somebody, do you expect to receive something good from them? We know the lame man was not offended simply by looking at His actions. Can people listen to your words and watch your actions and know you are not offended at God?

Just like the man by the pool, the lame man was healed because he was not offended. He had ample opportunity throughout the years to pick up an offense, but he did not give in to the temptation. Through the disciples, he was able to receive from God everything he needed.

How do we know the lame man was healed? The Bible tells us, "[I]mmediately His feet and ankle bones received strength. So he, leaping up, stood and walked and entered the temple." Whatever His ailment was, it affected His feet and ankles and now they were strong enough to walk on. He was physically healed.

Look at the next three words—"walking, leaping, and

praising God." Walking is the physical manifestation of His healing, so we know he was not offended. Can you picture this man in your mind? He had never been able to walk on His own. Never jumped. Possibly never even stood up. And now he is moving on His own and shouting praises to God. He's saying "Thank you, Lord. This is the most amazing thing ever!"

"Praising God" shows us that not only was he physically healed, but he was spiritually healed. We are three part beings—body, soul, and spirit. Jesus never healed anyone that He did not make whole, completely whole, not just fixing a leg or stopping an issue of blood. All the people He healed on earth were made whole—body, soul, and spirit.

So this man is walking and praising God on His way into the temple. People are watching him. They see the physical healing because he was the man they saw sitting, never walking, for years. And considering the shouts and hallelujahs coming from His mouth, they understood the spiritual healing. But what they didn't know about was the emotional healing. Read those verses again:

> So he, leaping up, stood and walked and entered the temple with them—walking, leaping, and praising God. And all the people saw him walking and praising God.

The people didn't see him leaping, did they? That's because the leaping was in His emotions or His soul.

Think about the woman at the well, broken emotionally and completely spent. Jesus comes along, and she is changed. She is not changed in just her body or just her spirit. She is changed in her soul. How do we know that? She goes back to the city and says, "There's a man out there who knows everything I ever did. He knows that I'm not with my husband. He knows I've been with all these guys over the years." Before she met Jesus, she never would have talked like that in front of other people unless her emotions were healed.

You can work your way through the Bible and study every person Jesus healed. He never partially healed. He always healed people all the way. When Jesus heals us, He does not want to heal just a part of us. He wants it all. He does not want to heal just your bursitis. He wants to heal your mind and the way you talk about your bursitis. He does not want to heal just the pain of rejection. He wants to heal the bitterness, the anxiety, the physical toll it took on your body—all of it, that's what He wants.

The people in Jesus's time wanted Jesus to change their physical circumstances and their economic circumstances. They wanted Him to take over the Roman government and eliminate the laws persecuting them, making them pay taxes, and holding them back. They wanted Him to change those things, but that's not what He was on earth for. He was here for a relationship with every person He encountered. He found the most obscure people in the most obscure places. He sat with them and heard all their pain, failures, and complaints. And then He told them all what He knew about them, and in the end, He said, "Now go and be whole."

Have you ever considered that God can heal all of it—the sorrow, the anger, the setbacks, the rejection, the hopelessness, the broken dreams—if you just sit with Him? Our expectation level as Christians in the kingdom is so low. Years ago, we learned in children's church that if we pray for people, they are physically healed. Yay, that's amazing! But we never considered that He can heal all of it, including our soul and spirit. Our expectation level about what we can do and what God can do through us limits God from completely healing us from offenses.

Maybe you have been walking with Jesus for fifty years; maybe you have been with Him for five months. Are you completely whole? Are you allowing God to heal every part of you? Or did you just receive a fire insurance ticket to get into heaven? I can guarantee one thing—If you are living in offense and letting the bitterness, anger, and sickness take over, you are not whole in God's eyes and not living up to your full potential in God's kingdom.

God wants a people who are completely whole, and when you become whole, just like the woman at the well, you want to take people back to the well. You become like the lame man, walking, leaping, and praising God. All you need is faith like the woman with the issue of blood in Mark 5:25–34. She touched the bottom of Jesus's cloak because the fringes on the bottom were called "wings" and the Old Testament said there is healing in His wings. She didn't need to go up to Jesus and hug Him. She just needed to have faith that if she touched the little fringes on the bottom of His cloak, she would be completely healed. Step out in faith and be made whole.

15

GUARANTEED PROVISION

L IVING A LIFE FREE OF offense doesn't mean life will be easy. We will always encounter problems and difficulties because we live in a fallen world. Satan will still tempt us, trying to get us to pick up offenses, but the choice is ours of whether we pick up the offense.

At times, living life free of offense may seem impossible; however, the Bible tells us that God provides whatever His children need. In fact, Revelation 1:6 tells us that God made us to be kings and priests. Everything a king needs is provided for him, right?

If you study the stories in the Bible about kings and priests, one detail you may not notice is that kings always went to war in the springtime. 1 Chronicles 20:1 says, "It happened in the spring of the year, at the time kings go out to battle..."

If you are anything like me, you're curious as to why kings went to battle in the spring. Not going in wintertime seems obvious, but what's wrong with summer or autumn? As I studied the battle stories, I dove into researching the significance of kings going to battle in the spring and why the Bible repeats many times that it was spring when the kings went out.

"But, Pastor Rob, this book is about offense, not kings going into battles." True, but Satan is going to hurl temptation after temptation at you, just like kings attacked their neighbors year after year trying to gain ground. You can choose to give in to Satan's temptation and pick up the offense, or you can rely on God to help you walk away from the offense. Here's what I discovered in my research…

1. Provision—During the winter, everyone ate the preserved harvest from the year before, but in the early spring, the first crops ripened. As the soldiers traveled and fought in the springtime, they found food along the way rather than having to pack and haul wagons full of food to feed everyone. When God calls us into battle, He doesn't say "Go without provision." Lots of times in our life, we decide we're going to battle, but the timing isn't right. When we get into battle, we discover that there's no provision and we feel defeated. However, God calls us at specific times to go to war, and when He calls His kings to go to war, the provision is always there.

2. Ripe harvest—Someone planted the seeds in the ground long before any of the soldiers arrived. Again, this goes back to God making sure the provisions were there and ready for the kings as they went into battle. God calls us to engage in battle and be prepared. He promises that if we follow, He will provide for us. The enemy misjudges us all the time. He thinks he can take ground away from God, but His timing is off. He can only defeat one person at a time, but God uses kings to bring armies to free many people at once. Even though you may be entering battle for the first time, God planned for you to take this path long before today.

3. Elements—We know from history that going to war in the winter can be devastating. (Read the story of General Washington at Valley Forge for a reminder of what winter

could do to armies.) The cold weather makes it much harder to move around, so the kings went to war in the warmer weather when they could be outside and not worry about the elements fighting against them. When we commit to ridding our life of offense, the battles we face aren't going to be like our previous battles. The elements, or distractions, will be gone. Those times that you went into your prayer closet and couldn't focus—gone. The times you tried to hit the target and missed—gone. When you make the commitment to be unoffendable, the timing, the weather, the provision—all of it—will be aligned and you will be victorious.

Some of us have everything we need to go into battle, and some of us have nothing we need. Some of us are in the best places, and some of us are in the worst places. It doesn't matter what our income level is. It doesn't matter what our comfort level is. It doesn't matter what our physical status is. None of those things matter. God doesn't care where we are and what we have. The only thing that matters is what our heart says. He wants a people who are ready to say, "I don't care what my physical circumstances are. I'm ready to do battle for the kingdom to reign on earth. I'm ready to look offense in the face and say 'No, not today. Not tomorrow. Not ever.'"

Not picking up offense may seem strange to you. It may look completely radical. It may be something that challenges you to your core. But…

Are you going to do what God is asking you to do?

Are you going to commit to living a life that is unoffendable?

ABOUT THE AUTHOR

ROB COBURN IS A SEASONED entrepreneur and the Lead Pastor of a thriving church in Dover, Ohio, and the visionary founder of One Summit Global. Throughout his dynamic journey as a leader, he has confronted and navigated numerous challenging situations, leaving behind scars and rough patches. Recognizing that some of these scars were hindering his personal growth, Robert embarked on a transformative journey to rediscover the fullness of the man he was created to be.

As he delved into the scriptures and initiated the healing process, Rob unearthed the resilience hidden beneath the baggage of his life. With a candid teaching approach, he now shares his experiences and insights to inspire readers on their own journey through the Word of God, encouraging them to live a life *UnCaught.*

www.ingramcontent.com/pod-product-compliance
Lightning Source LLC
LaVergne TN
LVHW041231080426
835508LV00011B/1155